# Endorsements

Occupational connections of most of the people offering endorsements are placed in parenthesis at the end their comments, identifying them by their involvement during the time of the history of tax base sharing. Non-Minnesotans Shayne Kavanagh and Anne-Marie Slaughter are identified by their current positions.

**John S. Adams**—"For 50 years Minnesota's 'fiscal disparities law' has worked well. Officials from around the country visit the Twin Cities asking, 'How in the world did this law get passed and implemented? And with what effects?' It's a fascinating story—well told by Paul Gilje—and will be of great interest to legislators, planners, local officials and active citizens struggling to match local government service demands with available revenues." (Professor of geography, planning & public affairs, University of Minnesota.)

**Tom Berg**—"A valuable explanation and compilation of tax-base sharing data, showing how an important fiscal tool came about and has worked in Minnesota for 50 years." (State legislator and U.S. Attorney, and author of *Minnesota's Miracle, Learning From the Government That Worked*. University of Minnesota Press.)

**Bill Blazar**—"This book delivers two for the price of one: an inside, detailed history of new tool for regionalism and a great case study of public policy innovation from inception to its adoption and implementation." (Senior vice president, Minnesota Chamber of Commerce, and a former research associate, Citizens League.)

**David Durenberger**—"Minnesota politics today is no model for the nation, State policy-making reflects largely the differences between Metro Minnesota (more precisely the Twin Cities) and Greater Minnesota - some of the metro suburbs and nearly all of non-metro. A sharp contrast to the times I served Governor Harold LeVander and Governors Elmer L. Andersen and Wendell Anderson. The Minnesota legislature earned a deserved national reputation with a State Planning Agency, a legal design for municipal incorporation, the Metropolitan Council and more.

"The most effective in the long run has been the work of Republican Chuck Weaver with DFL counterparts which by 1971 designed and passed 'Municipal Tax Sharing'.

"As a larger community Minnesota legislators knew economic development, which spurred state and local tax capacity growth, depended on changing economic factors affecting regional and state development. Also that the economic growth of all municipalities could/should benefit from these changes in a national and regional economy. The answer was tax sharing which I was pleased to have played a role in assisting Chuck Weaver and others in passing. I learned lessons from its successful implementation which followed me to my three terms of service in the US Senate and on its Finance Committee, Environment and Public Works Committee, and in Intergovernmental Relations." (U. S. Senator from Minnesota.)

**Curt Johnson**—"This is the best story ever of a complex but startling simple public policy that has measurable effects that are really all favorable. How many such policies can anyone count like that? It is one of Minnesota's often-admired but rarely-imitated initiatives done long enough ago to see what the results are. The ratio today between the wealthiest metro community, measured by tax capacity, and the least wealthy is much smaller than it would have been. Certainly some people don't like that, but it is good for this metro area and would be good anywhere it is tried." (Chair of the Metro Council, a former chief of staff to a governor, but also a writer who co-authored more than a 100 newspaper articles for more than 30 newspapers around the country, as well as author or co-author of 5 books.)

**Shayne Kavanagh**—"Minnesota's local government 'Fiscal Disparities' program is unique in the United States. Many people have asked how this program came into being and how it has worked. This book answers those questions with a one-of-a-kind, comprehensive historical look from the people who lived it." (Senior manager for research, Government Finance Officers Association.)

**Sean Kershaw**— "There is so much to learn from the history of tax-base sharing that is applicable today: most importantly the need to nurture the new generation of leaders who can work together on next generation of innovative ideas like tax-base sharing was fifty years ago." (Executive director of the Citizens League.)

**Gene Knaff**—"*How Could You Do This?* is a long-overdue history of property tax-base sharing in Minnesota. Almost 50 years ago individual citizens, Republicans and Democrats, from center cities and suburbs, met and crafted an innovative mechanism to share the growth in property tax resources among all local government jurisdictions in response to the local fiscal crisis. Operating within the existing property tax system, tax-base sharing respects local control, does not create or rely on a separate outside government entity and is also supportive of metropolitan-wide environment and development objectives.

"The book chronicles a fascinating process from the initial citizen-generated idea through the ups and downs of shepherding a relatively complex mechanism through the Legislature and, after passage, surviving subsequent court challenges including US and state supreme courts, and various attempts at repeal or major change. It recounts in detail significant citizens, legislators, researchers, and events.

"In addition, two important chapters lay out the context, a metropolitan area with numerous overlapping jurisdictions competing for property tax resources, and a blueprint for the initial citizen study that initiated the idea and followed through all the way to legislative passage. The importance of this vibrant citizen-engaged group, outside any government entity, was critical. Tax-base sharing does not eliminate "fiscal disparities" which remain an endemic problem in most US metropolitan areas, but it is relevant to improving local government fiscal health. Chapter 9 discusses base-sharing ideas examined in other metro areas, in past years as well as in 2020. Finally, there is a treasure trove of footnotes, publications, contacts and other reference resources.

"Not least of its benefits, the book harkens to a time when civic engagement and bipartisan political collaboration combined to successfully address common problems." (Research economist with the Metropolitan Council)

**Todd Otis**—"If you want to be inspired and reminded: inspired by smart, public service-oriented people and reminded that bi-partisan, pragmatic visionaries move us all the right direction. Earnest citizens conceived the idea; able politicians passed it into law; and a forward-looking Supreme Court upheld it. This is what governing should be all about." (Member of the Minnesota House of Representatives, public affairs consultant, and early childhood advocate.) He is a son of Justice James C. Otis, Jr., who wrote the majority opinion in the Minnesota Supreme Court, upholding the tax-base sharing law.

**Kaye Eleanor Rakow**—"The Mall of America's (MOA) attempt to divert money from the Fiscal Disparities Pool to subsidize their parking ramp is what prompted me to dive deep into understanding this obscure program. At the time I was the Director of Public Policy for NAIOP, the commercial real estate development association. Because commercial real estate taxes are the only source funding the pool, diverting money to pay for a competitor's parking ramp didn't sit well with NAIOP members as the legislation called for an increase in commercial property taxes to cover the MOA subsidy. Now many years later, I enjoyed reading the actual history of the Fiscal Disparities Pool and along with that, understanding so much about the fiscal history of the metropolitan area, which all history buffs will appreciate. Reading this history demonstrates just how much a group of committed citizens can accomplish when they put their collective minds to it. I'm certain elected and appointed officials will also reach a greater understanding of how citizens thinking creatively can develop policy and persuade elected officials to listen after reading this remarkable history. A good lesson for all of us." (Director of Public Policy for NAIOP, the commercial real estate development association)

**Andrew Reschovsky**—"In almost all metropolitan areas differences exist in the ability of local governments to meet the public services needs of their residents. These *fiscal disparities* create inequities and distort economic growth. *How Could You Do This?* tells the fascinating story of the development and implementation of metropolitan area *tax base sharing*, an innovative policy to reduce fiscal disparities without restricting the fiscal decision making powers of local governments. As the book clearly documents, tax base sharing has not only withstood the test of time but has inspired interest around the world." (Professor of public affairs and applied economics, University of Wisconsin-Madison)

**Lyall Schwarzkopf**—"Tax based sharing is one of the most interesting laws we passed in my 10 years as a state legislator. It took much cooperation from Minneapolis, St. Paul, and the suburbs to pass it." (Minnesota state legislator)

**Anne-Marie Slaughter**—"Municipal tax-base sharing is such an important idea, one that could address so many of the entrenched inequalities American cities and communities face. It is valuable and encouraging to have a concrete example of how it works and what it took to make it happen." (CEO of New America)

**Lori Sturdevant**—"*How Could You Do This?* puts a spotlight on one of several groundbreaking achievements during what is remembered 50 years later as the most innovative and fruitful policy-making period in Minnesota history. It's not an exaggeration to claim that legislatures and governors of the late 1960s and early 1970s, and the citizens on whose input they relied, made modern Minnesota. Their work is well worth studying, especially by those who seek to overcome today's partisan gridlock and restore inventiveness to lawmaking." (Editorial writer and columnist, Star Tribune)

# HOW COULD YOU DO THIS?

## 50 Years of Property-Tax-base Sharing in Minnesota

Paul Gilje

CENTER FOR POLICY DESIGN PRESS

ISBN 13: 978-1-7362007-2-8

Manufactured in the United States of America

First Printing: 2021
25 24 23 22 21    5 4 3 2 1

Cover and interior design by James Monroe Design, LLC.
jamesmonroedesign.com

CENTER
FOR POLICY PRESS
DESIGN

Center for Policy Design
332 Minnesota Street W1360
Saint Paul, Minnesota 55101
centerforpolicy.org

To those who believe in the necessity of real system change and who have labored to get new ideas discussed, modified, implemented, affirmed, and retained.

# Contents

Special Thanks. . . . . . . . . . . . . . . . . . . . . . . . . . . . . . . . . . . . . . . . . *vii*

Foreword. . . . . . . . . . . . . . . . . . . . . . . . . . . . . . . . . . . . . . . . . . *ix*

Introduction . . . . . . . . . . . . . . . . . . . . . . . . . . . . . . . . . . . . . . *1*

**CHAPTER 1**

Debating The Fiscal Implications of Metropolitanism . . . . . . . . . . . . . . . . . . . . . . 5

**CHAPTER 2**

Originating Tax-Base Sharing: Citizens League Committee . . . . . . . . . . . . . . . . . 23

**CHAPTER 3**

Enacting Tax-Base Sharing: Minnesota Legislature. . . . . . . . . . . . . . . . . . . . . . . . 41

**CHAPTER 4**

Implementing tax-base sharing: County cooperation was essential . . . . . . . . . . . . 67

**CHAPTER 5**

Legitimizing tax-base sharing: Three big lawsuits . . . . . . . . . . . . . . . . . . . . . . . . . 71

**CHAPTER 6**

Protecting tax-base sharing: Resisting efforts to reduce its impact . . . . . . . . . . . . . 87

**CHAPTER 7**

Enlarging tax-base sharing: Efforts to broaden its impact . . . . . . . . . . . . . . . . . . . 101

**CHAPTER 8**

Evaluating tax-base sharing: Everyone wins, ultimately . . . . . . . . . . . . . . . . . . . . . 111

## CHAPTER 9

Preserving tax-base sharing: Ongoing concerns and opportunities . . . . . . . . . . . . 119

## CHAPTER 10

Working outside the "givens": The broader effect of the Citizens League . . . . . . . 137

## CHAPTER 11

Changing tax-base sharing?: The future of metropolitan public finance . . . . . . . . 145

## CHAPTER 12

Honoring the heroes of tax-base sharing . . . . . . . . . . . . . . . . . . . . . . . . . . . . . . . . . 151

*Appendix* . . . . . . . . . . . . . . . . . . . . . . . . . . . . . . . . . . . . . . *159*
*Endnotes* . . . . . . . . . . . . . . . . . . . . . . . . . . . . . . . . . . . . . *169*
*References* . . . . . . . . . . . . . . . . . . . . . . . . . . . . . . . . . . . . . *185*
*About the author* . . . . . . . . . . . . . . . . . . . . . . . . . . . . . . . *189*

# Special Thanks

In chapter 12 we list about 70 "heroes" of tax-base sharing: originators, advocates, and opponents. But at the outset we want to express thanks to a few for their special contributions, specifically, in connection with preparation of this history:

- **Alan Dale Albert**, the Harvard undergraduate who in his unpublished 1978 thesis provided a fascinating and detailed account of the debate in the Minnesota Legislature over tax-base sharing. Our history relies heavily on Albert's work.

- **Ted Kolderie,** who wrote the foreword, who has been the author's mentor for more than 60 years, and whose leadership on tax-base sharing has continued unabated.

- **John W. Windhorst, Jr.,** the lawyer who drafted the tax-base sharing bill in 1969, who later represented the Metropolitan Council in defending tax-base sharing in the courts, and who has provided great help in assembling this history, particularly the section dealing with court challenges.

- **Steve Dornfeld**, who as a journalist covered tax-base sharing's passage in 1971, who was continuing to write articles for the media on the topic as late as 2013, and, in a very valuable role, spent two volunteer weeks proofreading this history.

- **Steve Hinze**, now retired from the House Research Department, non-partisan arm of the Minnesota House of Representatives, who since the mid-1970s—and particularly in connection with this history—has been an accurate, walking encyclopedia on tax-base sharing developments.

- **Dan Loritz,** who as senior fellow and president of the Center for Policy Design, has generously provided a "home" for our online history.
- **Jay Monroe,** newcomer in 2020, but just as valuable, for his work in design of our on-line history.

# Foreword

Paul Gilje has made a major contribution with his careful, dogged, research into the origins of this remarkable piece of public policy: the Minnesota Legislature's action to share among all the local jurisdictions in the region a significant part of the growth of the property-tax base of the Twin Cities metropolitan area.

This history is remarkable in all four ways revealed as the stress moves from one word to another in its title.

**'This'** . . . the decision to share not all but a part of the growth of commercial-industrial valuations; recognizing that—however enlightened the local planning—Nature's decisions about woods and hills and others' decisions about airports, freeways, parks and shopping centers also help shape the location of 'the local tax base'.

**'How'** . . . the ingenious suggestion to address the problems of disparity not by consolidating jurisdictions or with a program of state taxation and revenue-sharing but by moving the base—the dollars-of-valuation—itself.

**'Could'** . . . the shock, and the resistance, when outsiders managed to break conventional concepts in a policy area long reserved to the taxing and spending interests.

**'You'** . . . The Legislature, certainly, responding to a new idea; as with the House member from a well-propertied suburb who said to Rep. Weaver: "I plan to vote against this. But if you need my vote you'll have it". Mainly, though, a citizen-based policy process thinking creatively and able to persuade elected officials to listen. It is this latter 'You' that perhaps conveys the most important lesson: the importance of getting to the causes of problems–which the 'stakeholders' in any major issue-area are seldom willing to do. 'The problem', in this case, being the 'beggar-my-neighbor' practices of local jurisdictions; the incentive on localities to maximize taxable development and minimize the number of people requiring services. Now attracting people attracts valuation.

To change systems, institutions, it is essential to get to causes and to find a realistic way to make change. Public affairs is at risk of losing sight of this now, when the discussion of 'issues' consists mainly of deploring-problems and reaffirming-goals. Clarifying-problems and defining-goals is important . . . but by itself, without a How, 'caring a lot' and 'meaning well' does not produce institutional change.

Finally, it is good to see this book published and distributed—in the new ways now possible—by the Center for Policy Design. The innovative change in public finance its book describes *is* a fundamental system change; reflecting well the core belief of the Center's founder, Walter McClure:

> "Systems and organizations tend to behave the way they're structured and rewarded to behave. If you don't like the way they're behaving, you probably ought to change the way they're structured and rewarded."

I think you'll enjoy the book . . . and be impressed by the story it tells. It should be of significance and of use to states and urban regions all across America.

—Ted Kolderie

# Introduction

"How could you do this?"

No, the title of this book has nothing to do with a parent admonishing a child.

Myron Orfield addressed the question to Ted Kolderie a couple of years ago as they were reminiscing about a law enacted by the Minnesota Legislature in 1971. Kolderie, as executive director of the Citizens League, had been active in passage of the law in 1971. Orfield, a former legislator and director of the Institute on Metropolitan Opportunity at the University of Minnesota, was not present in 1971 but had been involved in analyses of the law and efforts to strengthen it.

They were talking about the law that guarantees every city in the Minneapolis-St. Paul metro area a share in growth of commercial-industrial property irrespective of where in the seven-county area the growth occurs. The law goes by the names "fiscal disparities" or "tax-base sharing". The term "fiscal disparities" has been in use for so long, it can't be dislodged. But the term is a misnomer. It refers to a problem, not a solution. As applied to the law, it should have been "anti-fiscal disparities". Since 1996 a similar law has been in effect among Minnesota's Iron Range municipalities.

Depending upon the emphasis given to different words, Orfield's question could be taken three different ways.

"How could you do *this*?" The questioner probably is wondering about the conditions in Minnesota that made it possible for such an innovative, pioneering, system-changing idea to be even suggested, let alone evaluated and enacted by a highly partisan legislative body.

*"How* could you do this?" The questioner probably wants to understand where the idea came from, how it received citizen endorsement, and how its advocates overcame inevitable legislative opposition.

"How *could you do* this?" The questioner probably believes that tax-base sharing is a bad idea. The book describes efforts to sidetrack the idea, in the courts, by citizens, legislators, city councils, consultants, governmental administrators, land developers and others.

Conditions in Minnesota that brought forth tax-base sharing are present across the nation, wherever municipalities and suburbs lie side-by-side in the same region. City councils, dependent upon the property tax for much of their revenue, compete with one another to enrich their property tax revenue base. Based on relative proximity to airports, highways, rail lines, and the availability of buildable land some municipalities always do better than others. The results are widely differing capacities to raise revenue, hence the term "fiscal disparities". It's not unusual for upper-income homes to be located in communities with more taxable wealth. Thus, differences amount and quality of public services can be substantial, again with the upper-income communities at an advantage. A recent scholarly article co-authored by Orfield helps illustrate the national problem of fiscal disparities[1].

By sharing 40 percent of net growth in commercial-industrial (C/I) property among all municipalities in the Twin Cities metropolitan area, Minnesota's law reduces, partially and gradually, differences in revenue-raising capacity, thereby reducing the rewards if municipalities deliberately try to attract certain development, such as shopping centers and offices, and discourage other development, such as low-income housing.

Curt Johnson, former Citizens League executive director, former chair of the Metropolitan Council, former chief of staff to Gov. Arne Carlson, and most recently with Citistates, a network focusing on metropolitan areas, has been in a position to examine other states' relative interest in tax-base sharing.

First, he notes that countless delegations from other states have visited Minnesota, eager to learn more about its innovation in metropolitan affairs, including tax-base sharing. But little action emerges, although this book highlights new developments that were occurring in 2020.

However, Johnson says, once enacted, tax-base sharing would seem to be immensely difficult, if not impossible, to be repealed, because the number of lower-valuation communities that experience net gain in tax base are substantially greater in number than higher-valuation communities that are net contributors.

So he asks this question: Wouldn't all metro areas in the nation be better off if they enacted tax-base sharing?

The following pages open by outlining fiscal implications of hundreds of independent units of government, side-by-side in a metropolitan area, followed by history of the idea of tax-base sharing, including pioneering work by a volunteer citizens organization. Next comes drama of legislative debate and decision, then valiant work by metropolitan area county employees to make the system operational. Following that is a description of three different challenges in the Minnesota Supreme Court. Then on to largely unsuccessful efforts to repeal, change provisions, or grant exemptions, with one exception. Activities in other states are listed, some ongoing to this day. Recognizing multitudes of public policy questions remain unresolved, we describe the citizen process that brought about tax-base sharing as a prototype. And we conclude with answers to six questions about the future.

# CHAPTER 1

## Debating The Fiscal Implications of Metropolitanism

### Can inter-municipal fiscal problems be addressed without sacrificing local control?

Municipalities side-by-side agreeing to work together rather than separately to provide certain services such as airports, sewage disposal, and public transit represent some of the earliest examples of addressing the implications of metropolitanism. Given the predominance today of Minneapolis-St. Paul International Airport it might be difficult to imagine that in the 1920s Minneapolis and St. Paul each had its own airport with scheduled airplane service between them.[2] The two municipalities with the help of the State Legislature created the Metropolitan Airports Commission in 1943.[3] Similarly, the two cities recognized their common interest in a cleaner Mississippi River and in 1930 received approval for a joint sewage disposal plant.[4] Inter-city transit, organized privately, got going in 1890 along University Avenue with the first streetcar line connecting the two cities.[5]

Another widespread approach, moving functions from the municipal level to the county level, has been quite common in Minnesota in areas such as health, criminal justice and courts.

Shifting financing to a higher, broader governmental level has potential to overcome differences in fiscal capacity at the local level, but such a result is not necessarily automatic. States could impose sales or income taxes to be levied on a metropolitan or state scale, with revenues shared on some basis. It's been common in Minnesota, to raise the money at the state level and appropriate specific dollars to local units. State aid to school districts has been around in one form or another in Minnesota since 1878, with major emphasis in 1957 and 1971 on equalization for differences in fiscal capacity.[6] In 1971 the Minnesota Legislature added a significant aid program for municipalities.[7]

Authorizing local units to impose their own sales or income taxes is common in many locations around the nation. In Minnesota several municipalities piggyback local sales taxes on top of the Minnesota state sales tax.[8]

Finding a way to give local units of government more equitable access to revenues without their yielding influence or power to higher levels of government has been difficult.

## We'd never think of making independent municipalities out of wards

It might be easier to understand the fiscal problems facing metropolitan areas by looking at the underlying structural nature of central cities. In Minnesota's largest metropolitan area, Minneapolis has 13 wards and St. Paul has seven wards, with members of their city councils elected from those wards. What if each of those 20 wards were an independent city, with finances of the "city" dependent upon what revenue could be raised within its borders? Imagine the fiscal differences between those with predominantly-residential neighborhoods with those that include the downtowns and the differences between the poorer and more affluent neighborhoods. No one would seriously suggest creating such disparities by dividing Minneapolis into 13 separate municipalities and St. Paul into seven separate municipalities.

The hypothetical illustration of dividing up the central cities isn't much different from the real example of financing and governing today's large metropolitan areas, each of which from the air looks like one city but whose "wards" are actually independent municipalities, with some lacking and some having a supply of higher-tax-paying property, but with each dependent upon revenue that it can raise within its borders. Depending upon their population distribution social costs will be higher in some municipalities than others.

## If residents are free to move from one municipality to the next, what's the problem?

The presence of C/I tax base is but one element in competition among metro area municipalities to attract and retain residents. To some extent municipalities treat residents as their customers, not just their voters or taxpayers. Within economic limitations, current and potential "buyers" decide to live in certain municipalities based on price and amount and quality of products offered by the "sellers", such as parks, water, sewer, streets, street-lighting, trash removal and amenities. In effect, when they choose where to live, buyers decide to accept higher or lower taxes based on the products offered. Then, as in private markets, if not satisfied with what they are getting for their money, they can vote with their feet and move elsewhere to acquire better products. Economist Charles Tiebout in the mid-1950s contended that the market of municipalities competing for residents could be a more accurate measure of quality in public services than is achieved via the political process. [9] In addition, many households and other interests want the advantages city life offers, but try to insulate themselves from what they see as city problems—like living next door to or down the street from low-income households and sending their children to school with children from families with different values and behaviors.

## One city or 190 municipalities in the same urban area?

Differences in fiscal capacity of municipalities in metro areas never would have emerged as serious problems if municipalities in the 20th century had practiced annexation of newly urbanizing development just outside their borders as they had in the 19th century.

In the 19th century as municipalities grew beyond their borders they typically annexed surrounding area. In 1854 Philadelphia consolidated with Philadelphia County, expanding its area from 2 to 130 square miles. In 1889 Chicago added 133 square miles. In 1898 with consolidation of its boroughs, New York expanded from 44 to about 300 square miles.[10]

Even during this time seeds of a change were emerging. What Kenneth Jackson calls "the first really significant defeat for the consolidation movement"[11] occurred in Brookline, MA, where many of Boston's wealthy elite lived. Dr. William P. Marchione, president of the Brighton-Allston Society, tells the Brookline story:[12]

> On October 7, 1873, the neighboring towns of Brookline, Brighton, and West Roxbury faced a momentous decision— whether to continue to be self-governing entities, or to relinquish their political independence to the City of Boston.

> The answers the voters of these three towns gave to that question were strikingly different. While Brighton and West Roxbury's endorsed annexation by large majorities, more than two-thirds of Brookline's voters emphatically rejected the opportunity to join Boston . . .

> Brookline's rejection of annexation took the wind out of a seemingly irresistible consolidation movement. Boston would, in fact, absorb no more towns for nearly forty years, until 1912, when Hyde Park became the last suburb to approve a merger . . .

> Of all the towns on the edge of Boston, Brookline was the most prestigious. In the late 18th century there had been little to distinguish it from its neighbors, but by the early 19th century this scenic and conveniently situated community on the southwestern edge of the city had emerged as its leading elite suburb.

Minneapolis and St. Paul grew by annexation during the 19th century, too. The Minneapolis south city limits—which initially stopped at Lake Street—were extended south in 1867 to 48th St., then in 1887 to 54th Street, and finally, in 1927, to 62nd St., which had been part of Richfield. St. Paul grew west from Western Avenue, to Snelling Avenue and finally, to the Mississippi River.

Among the 25 largest metropolitan areas in the United States the Twin Cities metro area today ranks second behind Pittsburgh, PA, in the most local governments per 10,000 residents.[13]

Complete merger into one city of all municipalities in the seven-county Minneapolis-St. Paul metropolitan area is unlikely ever to have been seriously considered. Minneapolis, St. Paul, Anoka, Hastings, Shakopee, Excelsior, and Stillwater are a few of many formerly-free-standing communities that gradually have become fully a part of the metro area.

In the late 1800s, St. Paul annexed what then were a few villages between the city's built-up sections and the Mississippi River, including Hamline and Merriam Park. Such action was not appreciated by Minneapolis, the growing metropolis on the other side of the river.[14]

In 1916 opposition from South St. Paul residents killed a proposal by the city of St. Paul to annex South St. Paul, in light of Armour Packing Company having announced plans for a new packing plant in the Dakota County suburb.[15]

The *Minneapolis Star,* on December 8, 1926, p. 1, offered insight into Minneapolis' hopes and reasons for wanting to annex all or part of several suburbs. The city of Richfield had just approved allowing Minneapolis to annex from Richfield the area between 54th Street and 62nd Street. "This is part of an extensive annexation program designed to increase the area and population of Minneapolis," the *Star* wrote, "and in this way lift it into still greater municipal importance . . . Other suburbs which annexation proponents hope will follow Richfield's lead and become part of Minneapolis include Robbinsdale, Osseo, St. Louis Park, Columbia Heights and Hopkins or West Minneapolis."[16] Perhaps most intriguing about Richfield is that it could have become one of the largest, if not the largest, city in the metro area had its 1858 boundaries as a township remained unchanged. The Hennepin County Board established in that year that Richfield Township would cover all the area between Lake Street on the north and the northern boundary of Bloomington (78th St.) on the south, and from the Mississippi River on the east to what is now Hwy. 169 on the west. That encompasses what is today all of Minneapolis south of Lake Street, all of Richfield, most of Edina, part of Hopkins, and St. Louis Park south of Minnetonka Blvd.[17] An 1886 partition of Richfield created the village of St. Louis Park, and a later division approved April 5, 1889, produced the village of Edina. Minneapolis absorbed sizeable portions of Richfield territory through legislative action or annexations in 1867, 1883, 1887 and 1927. The growth of Twin Cities International Airport during the last half of the twentieth century and addition of land to the Fort Snelling compound meant further reductions.

Ultimately, annexations by Minneapolis other than Richfield did not occur. Columbia Heights, led by a youthful mayor, undertook a multi-year annexation effort that finally was squelched by a Minneapolis City Council committee that recommended rejection. An obstacle was a $300,000 Columbia Heights debt that would have been assumed by Minneapolis.[18] Robbinsdale voters narrowly rejected annexation in a referendum.[19] A majority voted yes, but the majority was 109 votes short of a 60 percent approval that was required.

Across the nation after the 1920 census, rural-dominated state legislatures began increasingly to look unfavorably on uncontrolled annexation by central cities, and at the same time made it harder for cities to continue annexing while making it easier for developing areas outside central city limits to incorporate, according to retired University of Minnesota geography professor John S. Adams.

## City-county consolidation is more common nationally

The National League of Cities identifies about 40 city-county consolidations in the United States. Over the last 40 years more than 100 consolidations have been proposed and voters have rejected about three-fourths of them.[20]

## Bloomingville or Burnston

In the early 1960s, a fascinating annexation-consolidation proposal involved the Minneapolis southern suburbs of Bloomington and Burnsville.

Achieving a large tax base always has been high on city councils' agendas, to help keep tax rates in check. During the 1950s and 1960s giant electric generating plants were particularly attractive. None more so than Northern States Power Company's Black Dog plant (named for an

18th century Dakotah chief) in Burnsville township, south across the Minnesota River from Bloomington. Other than its power plant Burnsville still was a largely rural township just beginning to see urban subdivisions. Bloomington with 54,000 residents, using electricity from Black Dog, was the state's fourth largest city.

In 1961 the Black Dog plant was paying about 75 percent of Burnsville township's annual budget.[21] The plant was built in the 1950s and at $40 million was called "the largest investment of any single manufacturing plant in Minnesota."[22]

Taking advantage of Minnesota law that then allowed a city to annex up to 200 acres of an adjacent township simply with approval of the landowner, not the town board, the Bloomington City Council without advance notice annexed the power plant on August 22, 1961.[23] Bloomington also voted to ask the Minnesota Municipal Commission to approve a merger of Bloomington and the entire Burnsville township, which would create the largest city in land area in the state, with 65 square miles.

Within hours of learning of Bloomington's actions, Burnsville officials called a special meeting of the township board for August 23, (attended by 500 people), and voted to commence legal action to block the annexation and the merger.[24] On April 24, 1964, the Minnesota Supreme Court ruled against the Black Dog annexation, including this observation: "As far as Bloomington is concerned, it is apparent that the primary and probably the only purpose of the annexation was its desire to acquire additional taxable property."[25] The next month the Minnesota Municipal Commission—which a year earlier had rejected Bloomington's request to merge with Burnsville—approved Burnsville's incorporation as a village. As of 2019 the Metropolitan Council estimates Bloomington's population at 90,271, and Burnsville, 62,785.[26]

Northern States Power Company, Black Dog's owner, distanced itself from the controversy. "We would never have agreed, if we hadn't been convinced that Bloomington officials were sincerely interested in development of the two communities as one area," said J. Roscoe Furber, NSP vice president.[27]

A cynic might accuse Bloomington of being disingenuous about wanting to merge with Burnsville, caring only for the power plant's taxes. But merger could have been paramount for Bloomington, believing that Burnsville would be more interested in merger once the question of the power plant was taken off the table by annexation to Bloomington. Some 60 years after the fact one can speculate what might have happened had Bloomington and Burnsville merged. Instead of serving as a border, the Minnesota River would be running through the middle of the merged city. Would the river on both sides have become the enlarged city's front yard? Would residential, recreational, environmental, commercial and industrial results have been different for the merged city than has actually emerged?

## And along another river to the East

About the time that the Minnesota Supreme Court invalidated the Black Dog annexation, another tax-base-power-plant controversy emerged on the eastern side of the metro area. St. Paul was unsuccessful in enriching its tax base by trying to convince NSP to build a new plant near its border with Newport on the Mississippi River south of St. Paul.[28] NSP said the site was too small, that the 800-foot smokestack would interfere with takeoffs and landings at St. Paul Downtown Airport, and that higher water temperatures would interfere with sewage treatment further downstream. Instead NSP went ahead with its plans to build what at that time became the largest power plant in the Upper Midwest, in Oak Park Heights, on the Minnesota side of the St. Croix River, in Washington County. Citizen groups unsuccessfully challenged the plant's environmental and recreational impact.[29]

Ted Kolderie, who later was executive director of the Citizens League when the tax-base sharing proposal was developed by a Citizens League committee and enacted into law, in 1964 was an editorial writer with the *Minneapolis Star*. Kolderie wrote the following introductory paragraphs to his analysis of the St. Croix power plant issue:[30]

The most useful way to understand the controversy of the proposed Northern States Power Co (NSP generating plant on the St. Croix River is to think of it as essentially the same controversy now going on over the extension of the 'wilderness' area in northern Minnesota or over the purchase of the McKnight property in Carver County for the Hennepin County park reserve.

Not as a case, that is, of Wicked Utility Raping Lovely Valley, but as a conflict between the drive for major area-wide recreational sites and the determination of local people not to give up tax valuable property for (as they see it) someone else's benefit.

The plant was approved in 1965 and opened in 1968. Just as the Oak Park Heights plant was being completed, State Rep. Howard Albertson, chair of the House Metropolitan and Urban Affairs Committee, whose district included Oak Park Heights, told the Metropolitan Fiscal Disparities Committee of the Citizens League that he was considering an interim study of the impact of fiscal differences on different communities in the Twin Cities area. (Later that year Albertson appointed Rep. Charles R. Weaver to such a subcommittee.)

According to the March 14, 1968 minutes of that meeting:[31]

He (Albertson) referred back to the controversy in 1965 over the location of the NSP plant on the St. Croix River. At this time the taxes in Washington County were going up rapidly. The St. Paul Mayor sent a letter to him, as well as to the county board, pointing out that the St. Croix River Valley is a recreational valley for the metropolitan area and that the NSP plant should be on the Mississippi River in Ramsey County. Instead, Mr. Albertson sent a letter back agreeing that the St. Croix River Valley should be shared for recreational purposes by everyone in the metropolitan area, but if Washington County were going to share its recreational area then the industrial development which is located in the other parts of the metropolitan area has to be shared with Washington County.

# Early metropolitan area leadership

The question of excessive competition for industry was an important topic facing the Twin Cities metropolitan area in December 1964 when several state, metro and local agencies released preliminary proposals for guiding change, calling the document "4,000,000 by 2000!", a population projection still far from being realized in 2020, let alone 2000. One recommendation:

> Consider broadening the distribution of tax receipts from commercial and industrial activities as a means of eliminating potentially harmful inter-municipal competition for industry. Such distribution would permit local planning and programming to proceed on a more cooperative and objective basis, and stimulate the preservation and development of industrial sites that are best from the standpoint of industrial needs.[32]

The agencies called themselves "The Joint Program", and included the Metropolitan Planning Commission (MPC) (predecessor to the Metropolitan Council), the Minnesota Department of Highways, the planning and engineering departments of Minneapolis and St. Paul and the highway departments for Anoka, Carver, Dakota, Hennepin, Ramsey, Scott and Washington Counties, plus the federal housing and roads agencies.

When Joint Program's final report was adopted by the MPC on July 14, 1966, some members of the commission opposed a proposal to "lessen inter-municipal inequities through a redistribution of tax revenues . . . C. David Loeks, MPC director until July 1, declared some such equalization of tax base would be vital to the program's policy of controlling the location of new major employment centers. Otherwise, he said, communities would continue 'what they're doing now—fighting like hell for tax base'."
[33]

Awareness of the Minneapolis-St. Paul metropolitan area as an identifiable entity was nothing new. A metro transit system, albeit non-governmental, had been around since before 1900. There were metro agencies for sewage disposal (1933), airports (1943) and mosquito control (1958). The MPC was established by the Legislature in 1957. Major league sports advocates recognized that Minneapolis and St. Paul would only play in the minors unless they got together. The Citizens League in 1954 had recommended the establishment of a metropolitan parks authority, with jurisdiction within 25 miles of the central cities, barely two years after the League was established, and more than a decade before it dropped its suffix "of Minneapolis and Hennepin County".[34]

## An editorial writer's prophetic thoughts

Two years before he would find himself as executive director of the Citizens League and leading a research and study program that included a fiscal disparities committee, Ted Kolderie in 1965 was an editorial writer for the *Minneapolis Star*. On October 29, 1965, in the last of a five-part editorial pages series, he was sharing his thoughts on the problem of the local property tax in a metropolitan area:

> We need to break away from the tyranny of the local property tax . . . which is so tangible, so unequally distributed around the metropolitan area and so possessively fought over by the local municipalities that it can never become an adequate base for financing the area-wide public services we now want to develop.[35]

Toward the end of the article Kolderie outlined options for revenue:

> We might, of course, raise the new revenue for metropolitan services through (say) a 1 per cent tax on sales—levied either in the absence of a state-wide sales tax or as a local (metropolitan ) supplement to a statewide tax for state purposes . . .

> Or by taking into a 'metropolitan tax base' that new major commercial and industrial development which, though necessarily *located* in some particular municipality, does not *belong* in any real sense to that municipality.

## Metropolitan area mayors' tax study adds momentum

During the mid-1960s municipalities and school districts were working hard to find new sources of revenue. Financed by a $50,000 grant from the Dayton Company plus a high-powered group of advisors, a Metropolitan Mayor's Tax Study was undertaken in 1966, led by Oscar Littterer, senior economist, Federal Reserve Bank of Minneapolis. Francis M. Boddy, associate dean of the University of Minnesota Graduate School, was chair of the advisory committee. Boddy later served on the Citizens League Fiscal Disparities Committee.

After offering recommendations on non-property taxes, the report touched on the property tax, as reported in the *Minneapolis Star*, January 19, 1967:

> We believe, however, that there is a critical need for in-depth study of the property tax and its problems and shortcomings for the development of all means to improve the administration of this basic tax; to make such modifications as will make it more equitable and more suitable as a support for local government in the metropolitan area, and to remove or reduce the uneconomic and, to a degree, irrational competitive land use effects it now produces.[36]

Using the report as a base, the metropolitan mayors came up with their recommendations to the Minnesota Legislature for a gross earnings tax and three specialty taxes for municipalities in the Twin Cities metropolitan area.[37] The Legislature in 1967 enacted a three percent sales tax, earmarking some of the revenues for municipalities and schools.

## Regular surveys begin illustrating inter-municipal property tax differences

Specific numbers became available in early 1967 outlining for the first time differences in property tax burdens across the metro area, thereby drawing attention to the extent of fiscal disparities among municipalities. The Citizens League had conducted surveys in previous years, but only for Hennepin County. This was the first year that the survey included the entire metro area. The League continued such annual surveys for many years thereafter.

The report revealed that homestead property taxes on a home with a market value of $18,000 varied from a low of $392 in Sunfish Lake in Dakota County to a high of $698 in Mahtomedi in Washington County. Second lowest was Eagan in Dakota County, $413, and second highest was Circle Pines in Anoka County, $682.[38]

## Legislature enacts 3 percent statewide sales tax; creates Metropolitan Council

Two enormously significant laws were enacted by the Minnesota Legislature in 1967, just before the Citizens League Board of Directors approved the establishment of a Fiscal Disparities Committee.

A 3 percent statewide sales tax was enacted; food and clothing were exempt. One-fourth of the tax was dedicated to municipalities and school districts and most of the balance for property tax relief.[39]

The Metropolitan Council was created as successor to the Metropolitan Planning Commission. The law provided for the governor to appoint the members, 14 from equal-population districts, and one, the chair, at-large.[40]

Both laws had been recommended by other Citizens League committees, and both laws would have impact on the Citizens League Fiscal Disparities Committee's work. The sales tax itself and the formula for distribution of sales tax revenue would affect the committee's proposals for non-property revenue for units of government in the metro area. The Metropolitan Council's new influence over future growth of the metro area became part of the committee's rationale for sharing future growth in commercial-industrial tax base.

## Major conference in 1967 on metro area fiscal problems builds momentum for change

The Upper Midwest Research and Development Council, metro area chambers of commerce, and the Citizens League sponsored a conference at St. Thomas College in December 1967 on local government revenue problems.[41]

According to a background paper, "Metropolitan Reorganization: the Fiscal Side", prepared by Ted Kolderie, executive director of the Citizens League, for the conference,

". . . the first and most obvious fact about the fiscal system of the metropolitan area is the fragmentation of the property tax base which is the principal source of support for local government . . . The key question facing the community now as we begin to move toward the planning and development of this total urban area, is how to put the fragmented tax base back together again."[42]

To illustrate the problem of fragmentation, Kolderie speculated what Minneapolis would be like if its 13 wards were separate municipalities. The ward containing the central business district, for example, would not like to share its tax base with the rest of the city, he said.

Would the magnificent park system of Minneapolis ever have been developed, for example, if each of the outlying wards had been a legally independent municipality of its own residents, and forced to depend entirely on the tax base located within its own boundaries?[43]

## Major airport for Anoka County vetoed

Communities in Anoka County in 1968 were anticipating increased commercial-development because the Metropolitan Airports Commission (MAC) revealed it was considering a second major airport for the Twin Cities metro area.[44] But in 1969 the newly-created Metropolitan Council vetoed the MAC's proposal for an Anoka County site in Ham Lake township. As reported by the *Minneapolis Star:*

Before the rejection yesterday, Blaine Mayor M. E. Ramsdell called on the council to 'permit the normal economic development of the northern communities . . .

'Should the Ham Lake airport site fail to be selected through the Metro Council's action, we ask does the council intend to subsidize these communities?'

After rejecting Ham Lake, the council said it would seek legislative approval of a Citizens League bill aimed at easing competition for property-tax revenue in the metropolitan area.

Under the league plan, half of all non-residential increases of property value in Twin Cities area communities would be shared by the entire region.

A community that entices a big development, such as an airport, now gets all the tax benefits. Under the league proposal, half the tax benefits would be shared by all communities in the area. [45]

## What you pay in property taxes depends upon the value of what everyone else owns

Units of government help pay their expenses by imposing taxes on owners of property. No, not a tax on your clothing or other household goods (although even that was subject to the property tax years ago.) We're talking here about real estate property—land and buildings.

Taxes on property have been around a long time, well before the founding of the nation. The tax raises lots of money nowadays, more than $500 billion a year in the United States, mainly for local government.

Let's say your city council is deciding its budget for the next year. The council figures out how much money it needs from property taxes. Property taxpayers then are billed for their respective shares of that amount, proportionately, based on the value of their individual property.

How much you pay relates to whatever everyone else is paying. So if there are lots of big buildings for business and industry, your share is less than if there are mainly homes in your community.

Your understanding of this book will be enhanced if you keep this fact in mind: what you pay in property taxes is related to and dependent upon the value of other properties that everyone else owns in your community.

In non-metropolitan areas if people live, work, and shop all within the boundaries of the same community, property taxes on all property within the community support the services needed by the residents and businesses of that same community. The situation is vastly different in metropolitan areas of America today. Now it is common—perhaps the rule—for people to live in one community, hold jobs in a second, shop in a third, be entertained in a fourth, worship in a fifth, and so on.

Given the financial implications of today's metropolitan areas, the rules of the game are eminently clear to members of city councils, school boards or county boards. They know their budgets are dependent upon what taxable properties are located within their own borders. Even if desired development is simply across the street, but in another city, they receive no benefit. They have no choice but to seek to influence the size and nature of what they call the property tax base, or fiscal capacity, within their borders.

## Would urban development be different without a property tax?

As long as municipalities finance a significant portion of their budgets from locally-raised revenues—whether sales, income, or property taxes or other sources—they'll always figure in the local revenue implications of their land use decisions. If they rely less on local property taxes and more on local sales and income taxes, as is the case in some parts of the nation, local revenue implications of those sources are every bit as important as property taxes. Thus the fiscal implications of metropolitanism are present in all locally-controlled revenue sources.

## Early Minneapolis jealousy of St. Paul

An editorial on August 11, 1886, p. 4, by a clearly disgruntled *Minneapolis Tribune* illustrates antagonism over St. Paul's expansion:

> The TRIBUNE is not ashamed to have the fact realized that, apart from the protests of the inhabitants themselves, it was the chief objector to the annexation by St. Paul of the territory lying between the two cities. Neither city then needed an acre of this inter-urban tract, although more than half of it was tributary to Minneapolis. The TRIBUNE exposed the scheme in all its impudence . . . But, most of all, the people in the annexed territory will complain of increased taxes. The new assessment of St. Paul amounts to $82,843,491, of which $13,207,505, or nearly one-sixth, belongs to the territory recently annexed. These people, who live miles away from what is properly St. Paul, and who get no benefit whatever from inclusion within the city's jurisdiction, must pay heavy taxes on a valuation of thirteen million. This is a very fortunate thing for St. Paul, while it is exceedingly irksome to inhabitants of Hamline, Merriam Park, and other neighborhoods in the subjugated territory. It simply means that these neighborhoods must pay a heavier tribute to St. Paul than the Danubian provinces ever had to pay to Turkey. For all the good the connection does them, they might as well pay the money to

Chicago. Under their former village governments they could have secured greater advantages for themselves by far, for a quarter of the taxes they will be obligated to pay as part of St. Paul. They could well afford to pay an annual tribute of many thousands of dollars to be released from their present bondage. They are not realizing the full meaning and absolute truth of the predictions made by the TRIBUNE at the time of the annexation; and they would offer no such feeble resistance as they did then, if the subject were to be considered anew.[46]

# CHAPTER 2

# Originating Tax-Base Sharing: Citizens League Committee

## Everyone shares growth in the Twin Cities metro area

The Citizens League, a non-partisan civic organization that had its start in Minneapolis in 1952 but gradually expanded its horizons to the seven-county metro area, in 1969 proposed a game-changing idea, known as tax-base sharing. The idea first surfaced on December 12, 1968, during an informal chat at the Midway Pancake House, next door to the Lexington branch of the St. Paul Public Library, at the southeast corner of Lexington and University Avenues in St. Paul.

The Citizens League Fiscal Disparities Committee was meeting that night at the library to continue its consideration of how to address problems of wide differences in taxable wealth among some 190 communities in the Twin Cities metro area. The committee had been meeting weekly since early March of that year.

Some members felt the most urgent problem was inadequate revenues for schools and municipalities. Others felt it was wide differences, or disparities, among schools and municipalities in revenues and spending.

But a consensus was emerging on attacking another problem, different, yet not unrelated. Because of the nature of the property tax, city councils had no choice but to employ perverse incentives for planning their municipalities' futures. One tool, for example, was called "fiscal zoning", deliberately excluding certain development, such as lower-priced housing, because it didn't produce enough property tax revenue to cover the expenses of the services utilized by residents of such housing.

It was in that environment that a new concept—never before tried, anywhere—was advanced. What if all communities could share in the tax benefits of new growth wherever it occurs in the metro area, not only within the limits of their own individual borders? Incentives would change overnight. No need to zone out lower-priced housing, for instance.

During the informal pre-meeting gathering at the restaurant, F. Warren Preeshl, a municipal bond dealer, member of the Burnsville School Board, and member of the Citizens League committee, shared with a few others a three-page proposal that he had written some six months earlier. The memo outlined for the first time Preeshl's tax-base sharing concept. Excerpts from that memo:

> This proposal seeks to ameliorate the wide discrepancies in tax base among the various municipalities and school districts comprising the seven-county metropolitan area. A major reason for this discrepancy is the unequal impact of commercial and industrial development . . . this commercial and industrial tax base would be removed from the taxing authority of the component municipalities and school districts . . . Each municipality and the school district would know its assessed valuation as derived from homesteaded property within its district. Each municipality and school district would also be told its share on a formula basis of the total commercial and industrial assessed valuation in the seven-county metropolitan area. On the basis of the total of these two figures each municipality would establish its mill levy.[47]

Preeshl's proposal was discussed by the committee that night.[48] His idea offered an entirely new dimension of metropolitan finance. Many other options were popular in discussion: (1) Merging the metropolitan area municipalities into one big city. That would eliminate the tax differences and the municipalities. Not an appealing thought. (2) Moving selected local functions to a higher level of government, leaving the local municipalities to handle the rest. Who would govern the service decisions at a higher level of government? Who would decide which functions? Police? Fire protection? Street maintenance? (3) Imposing a new tax at the metropolitan level and distributing its proceeds to the respective municipalities. Much more attractive to the municipalities needing money to spend, but not so much to the taxpayers. (4) Direct aid from the state. This option would grow in coming years and, in 1971, along with tax-base sharing the Legislature enacted major increases in state aid to school districts and municipalities.

While the concept of tax-base sharing emerged at a time when municipalities and school districts were urgently seeking more funding, it became clear early on that tax-base sharing itself was no revenue panacea for municipalities or schools.

But Preeshl understood the real potential of his idea. It increased the capacity to raise revenue in hard-pressed lower-valuation communities, without diminishing the power of these communities to determine their own spending. He opened a new door, one that others had no idea even could exist. Municipalities could reach the wealth of the region without sacrificing local control.

With the exception of a similar approach in the Meadowlands area in New Jersey, across from New York City, tax-base sharing occurs nowhere but in Minnesota. Many states have studied the plan but haven't taken the plunge. In 1971 the concept applied only in the seven-county Twin Cities metropolitan area. Since 1996 it also has been applied on Minnesota's Iron Range.

Before 1971 residents of the metro area received tax benefit for commercial and industrial property only located within their respective city limits. Residents were likely to live in one city, work in another, shop in another, but receive tax benefit only for the job locations and retail establishments within their own city limits. That's the way the property tax system worked in every state. But in the Twin Cities metro area since 1971 residents have received tax benefit from commercial-industrial development wherever it occurs in the entire seven-county area. *That's right, everyone in the seven-county metro area shares in the growth of commercial-industrial property tax base, irrespective of where in the metro area the property is located.* If you live in Cottage Grove, for example, a city along the Mississippi River in southern Washington County, you can claim a share of commercial-industrial property in Maple Grove, in northwestern Hennepin County.

Everyone contributes; everyone shares. Technically, each city and township in the seven-county metro area contributes 40 percent of its net growth in commercial-industrial value (or "tax base" as the financial people would say) since 1971 to a metropolitan pool. The pool is redistributed to each contributing city and township, mainly based on population, with an adjustment up or down, depending upon whether the locality is below or above average in property tax value. School districts, counties, watershed districts and any other entities with property taxing authority also have access to the shared property tax base.

A superb description of tax-base sharing, comprehensive and clear, was prepared by Bob DeBoer of the Citizens League and Kaye Rakow of the Minnesota chapter of NAIOP (Commercial Real Estate Development Association) in 2007.[49]

## The Citizens League establishes a committee on fiscal disparities

The Executive Committee of the Board of Directors of the Citizens League in the 1960s was charged with bringing to the board annually a list of proposed study projects for the organization. The Citizens League staff, servicing the Executive Committee, would routinely prepare a list of 75 to 100 possibilities, of which fewer than 10 would be recommended by the Executive Committee for Citizens League study in the upcoming 12 months.

The Board of Directors approved a study on fiscal disparities on September 27, 1967. Excerpts from minutes of that meeting:

> The next project proposed to the Board was one dealing with metropolitan fiscal disparities. It was noted that this project as worded does not include any reference to a review of tax-exempt properties. It was moved, seconded and carried that this be included in the assignment. At length it was moved, seconded and carried that with this addition the proposal be approved. It would involve a consideration of measures to remove the inequities among various parts of the metropolitan

area and the changes in the system of local finance required by any effort consciously to guide development on the metropolitan level. The 1967 tax law would be reviewed; the current method of taxing electric generating plants would be reviewed; the feasibility and desirability of placing the resources of the area as a whole behind borrowings of local units will be included; and also the matter of tax-exempt property.[50]

Fiscal disparities was one of seven study projects recommended to the Board of Directors that day. The others: metropolitan development guide, Minneapolis city development program, strengthening the public service, water supply, public schools, and four-year college for the Twin Cities area.

The possibility of programming a fiscal disparities topic had been around for at least two years. A staff draft of possible research projects dated June 11, 1965, includes the question of addressing tax implications of inter-municipal competition for tax base.[51] It was not until the summer of 1967 that the project was recommended for study.

## Membership of the Fiscal Disparities Committee

Earl F. Colborn, Jr., a Minneapolis lawyer, who had chaired a Citizens League committee on property tax assessment reform two years earlier, was named chair. Some 54 Citizens League members volunteered to serve, of whom 29 participated actively in the deliberations. Their names, included in the final report, in addition to Colborn, were Arch Berreman, Francis M. Boddy, Bruce Brayton, Thomas Connelly, John Costello, Mrs. Nicholas Duff, Robert L. Ehlers, James C. Erickson, Julian Garzon, Loren Gross, State Rep. George F. Humphrey, Peter Meintsma, Gordon Moe, Thomas R. Mulcahy, Mrs. Harold Nash, Donald S. Nolte, Mrs. Vernon Olsen, Mrs. Stanley C. Peterson, F. Warren Preeshl, Thomas E. Reiersgord, State Rep. Martin Sabo, Arne Schoeller, Willis F. Shaw, Matthew H. Thayer, Thomas Vasaly, Donald Wahlund, Norman Werner, and Arthur Whitney.[52]

A few other members served on an early "Agenda Subcommittee", but were not present for deliberations. They included State Sen. Robert Ashbach, State Sen. William G. Kirchner, State Rep. Fred Norton, and State Sen. Roger Scherer.

Sabo, later to become a member of the U.S. House of Representatives, was a co-author on the tax-base sharing bill that became law. Several members were occupationally involved in public finance, including Boddy, Ehlers, Meintsma, Moe, Preeshl, Reiersgord, Shaw, Vasaly, Wahlund, Werner and Whitney.

## Excerpts from Fiscal Disparities Committee meetings

Lynn A. Stiles, senior economist, Federal Reserve Bank of Chicago:

Communities have frequently zoned to attract tax base and repel consumers of public services. This is known as fiscal zoning, in Mr. Stiles' words. A community will zone to bring in a new industrial plant, and the taxes raised thereby represent a net windfall to the community, since the amount of services required by the government because of its location there is very low . . . It must be kept clear that the culprit is not the property tax as such, but it is the fiscal autonomy of the governments side by side . . . The property tax would not be the culprit if the same rate were applied areawide. Then there would not be the incentive to locate certain properties in certain municipalities.[53]

John Pidgeon, Bloomington City Manager:

Mr. Pidgeon noted that one of the purposes of the Bloomington zoning code as specifically stated in the code is "the creation and protection of a tax base". No one will quarrel that in this day and age a local unit of government would be derelict if it did not take actions which are calculated to increase the tax base for its residents. To carry this into effect, of course, is a different question. Bloomington has developed very strict zoning, building and fire codes. By their very nature these standards require that developers invest more money than they otherwise would, which improves the taxes. By the same token, such codes may in some cases adversely affect the tax base, because industries would be inclined to locate elsewhere. This has occurred to some extent in Bloomington.[54]

Larry Laukka, vice president and marketing manager, Pemtom, Inc.:

There is a tremendous effort being exerted by the governing bodies of these various units (suburban communities) to keep out the lower valued housing.

The major reason for this action is simply the impact of the property tax. Local municipal governments, feeling the increase in taxes because of schools, believe that if they can hold the value of housing at an artificial high level they can effectively slow down the growth rate and keep out the rapid increase in school population.[55]

Rollin H. Crawford, mayor, West. St. Paul, with comment by Robert Ehlers and James Erickson, committee members,:

Mr. Ehlers questioned whether the fiscal disparities problem is holding back progress in the metropolitan area. He noted that even such poor communities as Lexington and Circle Pines are embarking on a sewage disposal program. Mr. Crawford pointed out, though, that the tax burdens fall remarkably heavy on those least able to pay which is in itself a disparity. Mr. Ehlers contended that municipalities follow certain cycles. Fridley, for example, went through a poor stage and has since developed a strong tax base. Mr. Erickson commented that the question isn't whether or not you provide a municipal sewage system, but it's the cost that a community has to pay for such a service as against another community. He also argued that the fiscal disparities problem prevents a reasonable approach to the open-space question because a county like Washington County must concentrate on attracting a tax base because it is forced to rely on the local property tax base only.[56]

## Staff memos compared differences in taxing, spending

An early staff memo was distributed to help committee members offer perspective on differences in tax rates and government and school spending. The memo included the following comparisons:[57]

- Percentage which property tax levy for debt service bears to total school district property tax levy: from a low (St. Paul) 10.4 percent, to a high (Rockford) 45.2 percent.
- Adjusted assessed valuation per pupil unit (1965) : from a low (Centennial) $2,311, to a high (Minneapolis) $15,608.
- Local property taxes for schools as a percentage of total school revenue receipts: from a low (Centennial) of 26 percent, to a high (Golden Valley) of 78 percent.
- School professional personnel per 1,000 pupils: from a low (St. Paul) 39.2 percent, to a high (Golden Valley) 63.8 percent.
- Net current expenditures per pupil unit: from a low (Anoka) $382, to a high (St. Paul) $541.
- Average salary classroom teacher: from a low (Rockford) $5,617, to a high (St. Louis Park) $8,697
- Estimated total property taxes on an $18,000 house (1968): from a low (Eagan) $296, to a high (Circle Pines) $492. In February 1969, the League conducted a similar study, this time on a $20,000 house, and for the first time adjusting the tax estimates for differences in assessment practices. Estimated taxes in 1969 ranged from a low (Inver Grove Heights) $293, to a high (White Bear Lake) $593.

The *Minneapolis Tribune* gave prominent coverage to the study, including a complete list of estimated taxes on municipalities in the metro area.[58] Such information might have had some effect on the Fiscal Disparities Committee's recommendations, which were under intensive discussion at that moment.

## Comparison of proposals for addressing fiscal disparities

When the committee began discussion of possible recommendations, six possibilities were on the table, A seventh was added on January 2, 1969, when the committee met to discuss the options.[59]

- **Preeshl**—Redistribute the commercial-industrial *tax base* among all school districts in the metro area.

- **Clay**—Increase and redistribute commercial-industrial property tax revenue to bring school districts with below-average tax rates up to the average.

- **Graven-Boddy-Thayer-Preeshl**—Impose a uniform tax rate on commercial-industrial property throughout the metro area for schools, replacing the tax rates individual school districts impose on such property. Combine the revenue with state aid earmarked for the metro area school districts and distribute the combined revenue to metro area school districts by formula. Also impose a metro area income tax with revenue designated for schools and, for a few years, to municipalities with extraordinary municipal tax burdens.

- **Advisory Commission on Intergovernmental Relations (ACIR)**—Largely the same as Graven, etc., above, with a provision for additional aid for school districts "with a disproportionate share of socially and culturally deprived students" and for school districts in municipalities where property-tax burdens for municipal services are unusually high.

- **Weaver**—Share one-half of the property tax revenue from large commercial-industrial developments through the existing formula for distribution of state school aids or for districts with extraordinary debt service burdens.

- **Metro Section, League of Minnesota Municipalities**—Impose a new gross earnings tax on residents of the metro area with 50 percent of the revenue for schools, 33 1/3 percent for municipalities, and 16 2/3 percent for counties. School districts would receive aid with special provision for disadvantaged and handicapped students.

- **Colborn**—Taxes on additions to commercial-industrial tax base and increases in value to this base, would be collected at the areawide level and distributed back to the local units of government. Taxes on existing commercial-industrial value would stay local. A new non-property tax, probably income, would be imposed to avoid further property tax increases.

# Reaching consensus in the Citizens League Committee

Thanks to thorough staff minutes—the result of incredibly valuable clerical staff speedily transcribing dictation from professional staff—an immensely detailed record exists of four Citizens League Fiscal Disparities Committee internal discussions between December 12, 1968, and January 23, 1969.[60]

One can't re-read these minutes without thinking that members of the committee were earnestly seeking a good solution, that they didn't appear to have strong ideological positions nor were their political views dominant. They seemed to have an excellent grasp of "fiscal disparities" problems, and, they knew it was important to develop specific recommendations on how the problems should be addressed. It wouldn't be enough for them to express the hope that differences in tax resources needed to be reduced. They needed to come up with enough specifics so that a bill could drafted in the Legislature to implement the report.

It didn't seem to take long, according to the minutes, before committee members realized that radical "surgery", say, merging municipalities, wouldn't be necessary to address what could be done to reduce municipalities' temptations to continue or increase fiscal zoning or implement other devices strictly to enhance tax base. Thus, it wouldn't be necessary to move existing tax base from one community to the next. Just concentrate on the location of future tax base, which no one knew absolutely for certain where such development would be located (although those communities expecting a lion's share of future growth made no secret of their opposition).

The committee sensed that tax-base sharing, while a good approach to address fiscal zoning, would not be an adequate response to the need of municipalities and school districts for more revenue. Consequently, the committee found itself largely in agreement to propose a non-property revenue source for local governments. The committee anticipated the same sort of "fiscal disparities" could afflict the metro area if each individual city were authorized to impose its own sales or income tax. Thus, the committee moved to recommend that any non-property tax should not be imposed on anything less than the metropolitan area as a whole.

Well aware of the enormous investment coming from electric utility plants, the committee concluded that such plants be taxed on a gross earnings basis, not by the property tax, with all revenues returned to local governments.

At the close of the meetings of internal discussion, on January 23, 1969, the minutes reveal that based on the discussions the staff should now prepare a draft report for consideration by the committee.[61] This was the final meeting at which minutes were recorded. Based on memories of staff members from the 1960s, the additional time required to prepare drafts of reports meant that no time was available to record the minutes. Between January 23 and March 12, when a final report was submitted to the Board of Directors of the Citizens League, we have no record of how many drafts were necessary.

## Final recommendations of the committee

Here are the recommendations taken verbatim from the final 32-page report of the Fiscal Disparities Committee:[62]

"Distribution of the Property Tax Base

"Let each locality in the Twin Cities area keep the tax base it has now. In coming years as the tax base of the area grows, give each locality access to a part of the growth of the tax base in the entire area, regardless of how much of that growth actually occurs within its own boundaries. In effect, no one loses anything he has now, and everyone shares in the growth.

"To accomplish this goal, the Legislature should change the property tax system so that one-half of the increase in non-residential valuation from now on will be shared by all units of government in the Twin Cities area, probably on the basis of population. The other one-half of the increase in non-residential valuation, plus all of the increase in residential valuation, would continue to be taxed exclusively by the units of government where the property is physically located.

"Non-Property Revenue for Local Government

"Provide a way for local government to obtain a new non-property source of revenue. If the Legislature authorizes 'local option' non-property taxes throughout the state, it should recognize the particular problems in the Twin Cities area and treat the area with a single policy to the greatest extent possible.

"Modify state aid to school districts to provide special aids for programs designed for educating disadvantaged children.

"Bonding

"Modify the current state law relating to special state assistance to school districts with heavy bonding requirements, perhaps by broadening eligibility for state assistance and by having the state guarantee bonds rather than issue them itself.

"Taxation of electric utilities

"Replace the property tax on privately owned electric utilities in Minnesota with a gross earnings tax. Distribute all gross earnings revenue back to local government.

"Research Data

"Improve data-gathering procedures by state administrative agencies to assist in tax research."

## Board consideration and action

The Citizens League Board of Directors spent three meetings in March 1969, on the 5th, the 14th and the 20th, considering the Fiscal Disparities Committee final report. The report ultimately was adopted by the Board on the 20th by voice vote without dissent.[63]

Minutes of board meetings were as detailed on content as were the committee minutes. The board spent most of its time on reviewing and acting on Citizens League reports, not on personnel, finance or other organizational matters. Board minutes are part of Citizens League archives, accessible through the office of the League.

Francis M. Boddy, professor of economics at the University of Minnesota, presided as president of the Citizens League. Boddy also served as an active member of the Fiscal Disparities Committee. Boddy's obituary, *Minneapolis Tribune*, March 21, 1983, takes note of his activity on public finance and his work with the Citizens League:

> An expert in state and local finance, Boddy was consulted
> by DFL and Independent-Republican governors from Orville

Freeman in the 1950s to Al Quie in the 1980s for help with matters ranging from tax studies to economic forecasts.

Boddy was active in the Citizens League, serving as president in 1968-69 and participating in virtually every one of its committees on public finance.[64]

Boddy is quoted frequently in minutes of the Fiscal Disparities Committee. At the March 14 Board of Directors meeting he yielded the chair to another board member to speak in favor of the committee's report.

The March 5 meeting provided background on the report, but no action was requested, because the Fiscal Disparities Committee still was winding up its work. A draft report had been mailed to the board on March 11, but the committee did not finally adopt the report until 9:45 p.m. on Thursday, March 13.

The board made a few technical changes in the report. Considerable time was spent listening to a minority report from committee member Robert Ehlers and discussing how the report should be handled.[65]

His dissent ran for 23 pages, 19 of which had been written in early January, two months before the report was finalized. He declined to condense his report, as requested by board members. The board decided to make the full report available on request at the Citizens League office, to include a statement in the report itself that listed two other committee members, Willis F. Shaw and Arthur Whitney as concurring in Ehlers' dissent, and to summarize the dissent. Ehlers' report expressed opposition to:

> A. Sharing the growth of commercial-industrial valuation—"This recommendation, if adopted, would severely harm those communities which are in the expensive formative stages and whose development will be **new** as opposed to those communities which already have their industries and commercial establishments on the tax rolls. It will be especially unfavorable to the core cities whose only hope for growth in tax base is, not in residential growth, but in construction of new industrial and commercial growth."

B. Non-property taxes as a substitute for additional property taxes for local government—"Property taxes are not so high as to require new replacement taxes."

C. A gross earnings tax to replace the property tax on electric utilities—"It is not true that the 'possessors' of this valuation receive a bonanza or a clear bonus in that local school aids in those districts (which levy most of the taxes in a community) are sharply reduced and additional school aids are thus made available to those communities which do not have such plants."

Board members present when the report was approved were Charles Backstrom, Dr. Francis M. Boddy, Fred C. Cady, Homer A. Childs, Earl F. Colborn, Jr., John A. Cummings, Mrs. Nicholas Duff, Harold D. Field, Jr., Mrs. Ralph Forester, Greer Lockhart, Charles Lutz, James Martineau, Donald W. McCarthy, John W. Pulver, Peter H. Seed, Paul Van Valkenburg, and John W. Windhorst. Robert Ehlers, Tom Anding and Gordon Moe are listed as guests, and Paul Gilje, Jim Carney, and Neill Carter, Staff

## Communicating a complex idea without PowerPoint slides

In the late 1960s personal computers were still unknown as were PowerPoint slides, of course.

But this didn't deter Ted Kolderie, executive director of the Citizens League, an ex-journalist experienced in communicating ideas understandably, from putting together two sets of "slides" on 8 1/2 x 11 paper, illustrating tax-base sharing step-by-step, one with 14 sheets and the other, 16 sheets.[66] Those packets were helpful with presentations to groups. Other mimeographed memos helped with one-on-one explanations.

## What's different about tax-base sharing from revenue sharing?

When the Fiscal Disparities Committee met on January 2, 1969, to evaluate various proposals, the fundamental new direction—redesign, if you will—that existed in the Preeshl idea was alive, but certainly not yet recognized for its significance. It's difficult to get one's mind around a new concept. Far better to try to fit that concept into what one already understands to be the situation.

Furthermore, the question of new sources of revenue for municipalities and school districts, within the metro area and statewide was much more on the minds of local government officials than was tax-base sharing. And tax-base sharing did not represent a new source of revenue. The Fiscal Disparities Committee developed recommendations on both tax-base sharing and a new source of revenue.

To understand Preeshl's approach to addressing fiscal disparities, it's vital to know where he was coming from. Not unlike others, Preeshl wanted to give each unit of local government in the seven-county metro area some access to the commercial-industrial wealth of the entire metro area. He wanted to accomplish that objective without some higher level of government imposing a tax and distributing the proceeds as it sees fit. He wanted to preserve the authority of local governments to set their own budgets and decide their own level of property taxation. Preeshl's idea also contained a built-in restraint on spending. Taxing jurisdictions would not be able to impose excessive taxation on commercial-industrial property, for the same reason as in the past: their local taxpayer-voters would bear the same rate as non-voting commercial-industrial owners.

What does *not* change under Preeshl is the authority of a county board, a school board, a city council, or a township board to decide how much revenue from their assigned *tax base* that these units officially seek(that is, levy, in the professional jargon) every year. Legal requirements are present as to what constitutes the *tax base*, such as some property being declared tax-exempt.

Until the Preeshl concept was enacted all *tax base* had to be physically located wholly within the physical confines of the township, city, school district, or county. In fact, most people likely could not imagine how a city council, for example, could ever include in its *tax base* property outside its borders.

What also did not change under Preeshl was that the portion of *tax base* attributed to a local unit of government as of the present day(or as the law now provides, as of 1971, the year the law was enacted) consists only of property physically located within the geographic limits.

Preeshl changes only the growth in commercial-industrial *tax base* from the time the law passed and going forward. It left the existing *tax base* as of 1971 unchanged. The future *tax base* of a local government within the seven-county metro area was no longer to be located exclusively within its geographic limits.

Since 1971, 60 percent of a local government's growth in commercial-industrial tax base, all of its pre-1971 commercial-industrial tax base, and all residential tax base remains where physically located. The remainder, 40 percent of the growth in commercial-industrial value, is shared by all units of local government in the seven-county metro area.

At this point in the process some persons undoubtedly will wonder how the revenue from the shared tax base gets into the treasuries of local governments. The owner of commercial-industrial property receives a two-part tax statement. The same tax rate as is applied to all residential property also applies to the portion of commercial-industrial property that remains local, which varies from municipality-to-municipality but in 2020 is a little bit more than 60 percent of property value. A uniform metropolitan-wide tax rate, derived as a weighted average of all local tax rates, is applied to the portion of commercial-industrial property that is shared, which in 2020 is a little bit less than 40 percent of property value.

Eagle-eyed readers at this point might say that the effect of tax-base sharing results in revenue sharing, and they would be correct. But the revenue that is shared is derived from local taxing decisions and is not determined by a higher level of government.

A key aspect of tax-base sharing is that it functions automatically year-after-year with no annual or biennial appropriation. The shared tax base is simply 40 percent of the net growth in value of commercial-industrial property since 1971. Conceptually, a different approach could have been undertaken, with the Legislature imposing a direct state tax on commercial-industrial property, and distributing the proceeds as the Legislature would decide in every biennium. Imagine the controversies that would exist if amounts were determined and appropriated every biennium in the legislative-political process.

## Newspapers reported extensively on Citizens League

In the 1960s newspaper coverage of Citizens League activity was extensive, and competitive. Citizens League reports when approved by its Board of Directors and released to the public, were well covered, as were other Citizens League activities. The Fiscal Disparities report, issued publicly on March 26, 1969, received immediate lengthy coverage.[67] That same month other coverage included news articles about at least four speakers at Citizens League breakfasts, plus editorials and letters to the editor on other subjects.

Enterprising reporters also managed to get under the skin of the Citizens League. On at least one occasion, in 1963, a reporter published a Citizens League report before the report was formally and released to the public. The subject was rebuilding needs of Minneapolis public schools. The committee studying the issue had submitted its report to the Board of Directors, but before the Board met, a committee member shared a copy with the reporter, whose article appeared the next day.[68]

# CHAPTER 3

## Enacting Tax-Base Sharing: Minnesota Legislature

### Several accounts of legislative action, led by unpublished Harvard thesis

Several accounts detail the events from March 26, 1969, when the tax-base sharing proposal was made public, to July 23, 1971, when the plan was signed into law by Gov. Wendell Anderson.

A thorough account, covering background on the plan's origin plus the process and politics in the Minnesota House and Senate, appears in a 2007 "Scholarship Repository" in the University of Minnesota Law School, by Myron Orfield and Nicholas Wallace.[69]

Ted Kolderie outlines the major events concisely in his book *Thinking Out the How*, including selected significant matters likely known only to him, such as "When the bill came up in the first special session Weaver got it through It was a fascinating vote; quite rational. Not at all on party lines. Rep. Lon Heinitz, from a well-propertied suburb, told Weaver he would vote 'no' if he could; but 'if you need my vote you'll have it'."[70]

In his book *Metropolitics A Regional Agenda for Community and Stability*, The Brookings Institution, 1997, Myron Orfield, University of Minnesota law professor, describes his efforts as a Minnesota legislator to strengthen the law as well as outlining sources of opposition.[71]

The Citizens League devoted its July 1971 newsletter to history and passage of the act.[72]

Thomas K. Berg, former member of the Minnesota House of Representatives, includes tax-base sharing in his book *Minnesota's Miracle*, 2012, as part of a package of tax and local government acts enacted by the 1971 Legislature.[73]

A history written by Alan Dale Albert, an undergraduate student at Harvard College in 1978-1979 might well outshine them all.[74] Albert in 1978 was a 23-year-old senior at Harvard, working on an honors thesis for his two majors, government and economics. In his search for a topic encompassing both majors, he came across information about tax-base sharing in the Minneapolis-St. Paul metropolitan area. With a $500 grant from the Kennedy School of Government at Harvard, he spent six weeks in the Minneapolis-St. Paul area in the summer of 1978, interviewing some 40 individuals who had been part of the tax-base sharing debate. Albert then wrote an unpublished thesis running some 250 pages, earning himself *magna cum laude* honors at Harvard. Albert went on to earn a master's degree at Oxford and a law degree at Harvard. As of 2020 Albert was a partner in the O'Hagan Meyer law firm in Richmond, VA.

## Key metro leadership from Rep. Charles R. Weaver of Anoka

"One would hardly have expected Anoka Conservative Charles R. Weaver to become a driving force at promoting legislation which was as metropolitan-oriented as the Fiscal Disparities Act," Albert wrote. " . . . The district, like much of the northern suburban area, was relatively poor in tax base. The northern suburbs had shared little of the commercial and industrial development which had followed the freeways, airport, and stadium southward . . . Weaver saw the development control authority of the new Metropolitan Council as one more means by which the southern suburbs might profit at the northern suburbs' expense . . ."[75]

# Important lunch date in November 1968

Albert describes a lunch date in November 1968 between Weaver and Ted Kolderie, executive director of the Citizens League, in which Weaver outlined his fiscal concerns that led him to oppose further development controls of the Metropolitan Council. Growing out of that lunch Weaver penned a letter to Kolderie, November 7, 1968—more than a month before F. Warren Preeshl's proposal for tax-base sharing was shared with the Citizens League—that prophetically suggested "a system could be devised to share part of the return from industrial and commercial development to the areas that are in need . . . to reduce the competition for industry at least to the point where it would be done with more objectivity but would still retain some incentive for local units of government to encourage a healthy balance of commercial and industrial growth . . ."[76]

Weaver also shared his concerns with State Rep. Howard Albertson of Stillwater, chair of the House Metropolitan and Urban Affairs Committee, and veteran of the King power plant controversy. Albertson formed a subcommittee, with Weaver as chair, to "deal specifically with problems of tax base disparity among localities".[77] The subcommittee first listened to metro area municipalities urge new non-property taxes for metro area local governments.

Albert: "Weaver was convinced that the prevailing political forces were such that reaching agreement on both collection and distribution of a new metropolitan area revenue source 'just wasn't going to happen,' . . . Finally . . . the Citizens League released its base sharing proposal."

Albert: "Weaver was immediately attracted to the sharing idea. First, and unquestionably foremost, it would help the tax-poor dormitory communities which made up his legislative district . . . Weaver was also strongly attracted to the proposal's preservation of local decision-making. No new taxing district or bureaucracy would be required to implement the plan, for it was 'automatic.' . . . No new source of revenue would be required."[78]

Possibly concerned how the suburb of Bloomington might be treated in upcoming legislation, the Bloomington City Council passed a resolution requesting "a two-year study by the Minnesota Legislature to determine whether property-tax resources are unequally distributed." The resolution was passed two months before the Citizens League made its tax-base sharing recommendation. However, officials of Bloomington were receiving minutes of the Citizens League Fiscal Disparities Committee and could have become apprehensive about how possible recommendations under discussion would affect their city.[79]

## Drafting the bill

Tax-base sharing isn't so difficult to explain in general terms: Everyone contributes and everyone shares, or every community in the metro area receives a share of commercial-industrial tax base, irrespective of where that tax base is located.

Even if the full explanation is a bit more detailed, it's still understandable: 40 percent of all commercial-industrial value in the metro area since 1971 is placed in a pool of valuations and redistributed to all municipalities and townships in the area.

But try expressing that idea in state law. Then it gets really dicey. After Weaver's Fiscal Disparities subcommittee met with the Citizens League for an explanation of tax-base sharing, Weaver asked the Revisor of Statutes office, the entity that drafts bills for the Legislature, to prepare a tax-base sharing bill.

Albert: "The task fell to John W. Windhorst, Jr., a young lawyer whose father had been active in civic affairs and was a senior partner in one of Minneapolis' largest law firms. (The elder Windhorst was a member of the Citizens League Board of Directors that approved the tax-base sharing report.) . . . Windhorst took the decidedly nontechnical Citizens League proposal and clothed it in technical language as best he could. While his initial draft was not perfect, Windhorst's expertise is evidenced by the relatively small number of technical amendments which were required to make this extremely complex proposal reasonably workable."[80]

Windhorst's language remains in the law to this day. Anyone familiar with tax-base sharing's inner workings can be grateful for Windhorst's ability to express, concisely and correctly, the many steps required (readers are free to skip the rest of this paragraph): excluding from the local tax base 40 percent of net growth in C/I, reassembling the excluded portions as a metro-wide pool, redistributing the pool back to the localities, attributing the correct amounts to overlapping taxing districts, assembling the levies from all units of government (municipalities, counties, school districts, and other units) on the metro pool of valuations, calculating the areawide tax rate on the pool, imposing that tax rate on each parcel of C/I property, collecting the taxes as imposed, and distributing the revenue to the appropriate local governmental units.

During legislative consideration Citizens League leaders urged people not to try reading the bill line-by-line, but instead to pay attention to reliable testimony and written examples. Sen. Jerome Blatz was opposed on policy grounds but also repeatedly claimed he couldn't understand the bill. "I have spent a lot of time on this bill and I can't understand it. Whoever drafted it apparently wanted to hide its message."[81]

## Finding authors for the bill

For co-authors Weaver sought balance in many respects, Minneapolis-St. Paul, central city-suburban, likely tax-base "winners"-likely "losers", Republicans-DFL.

Albert: "Weaver's choice for Minneapolis co-author was clear-cut; DFL minority leader Martin O. Sabo had served on the Citizens League Fiscal Disparities Committee which produced the base sharing proposal, as well as on Weaver's subcommittee. Moreover, Sabo was an effective, highly-respected leader among DFLers. St. Paul was represented in the person of Conservative Joseph T. O'Neill and, for eastern suburbs, Albertson. Finally, Weaver enlisted the sponsorship of Conservative William E. Frenzel, who represented the western suburbs of Golden Valley and St. Louis Park and had been a strong proponent of a directly-elected Metropolitan Council . . ."[82]

## House committee action in 1969

In retrospect it would have been unusual that any action whatsoever could have occurred in 1969. The Citizens League report wasn't even announced publicly until March 26, and the Legislature adjourned less than two months later. It was astounding, therefore, that the bill sailed through the House, was moving in the Senate, and only died when Donald O. Wright, Minneapolis Conservative and Senate Tax Committee chair, cancelled a scheduled hearing.

Albert: "Weaver introduced the bill on April 21, 1969. He had little trouble in persuading his subcommittee to endorse the bill and send it on to the full Metropolitan and Urban Affairs Committee for its consideration. There, he found surprisingly broad support for the measure. Rep. Salisbury Adams, Wayzata, a crusty, influential suburban Conservative who had chaired the House Committee on Commerce and Economic Development since 1967, spoke glowingly of the bill's ability to 'moderate the business of shopping for tax shelters' practiced by many industries . . . [83]

On Frenzel's suggestion the committee amended the bill to change the provision for sharing 50 percent of C/I growth, as recommended by the Citizens League, to 40 percent. Frenzel advised Weaver that for strategic reasons it would be good to assure all municipalities that they would be guaranteed at least a majority of their C/I growth, plus, of course, whatever they would receive from the metro pool.

Albert: "Weaver agreed; he saw the move as an excellent means of 'pouring water' on the arguments raised by some opponents that, under base-sharing, new development would no longer pay for the additional service costs it entailed."[84]

Albert: " . . . only two committee members expressed strong objections to the measure: Rep. Joseph Graw (C-Bloomington), who was particularly incensed by the unavailability of information as to the bill's impact, and DFLer Thomas Ticen, also from Bloomington, who tried to kill the bill by seeking re-referral to the House Appropriations Committee. Their objections were largely ignored . . . and instead on May 3 the committee passed it on to the full House . . ."[85]

## House floor action in 1969

During floor debate two amendments were defeated. One offered by Graw would have referred the bill to the Tax Committee. One by Rep. Carl Moen, Fridley DFLer, would have shared pre-1971 C/I as well as growth. The bill passed the House on May 16, 115-14, by far the largest margin of approval for any tax-base sharing vote in either House or Senate, in 1969 or 1971.[86]

Albert: "Opposition to the bill was largely confined to suburbs which perceived themselves as net losers under the plan; fully ten of the fourteen who voted against the bill represented suburban districts. The vote, however, was to some extent a 'casual' one. It came so late in the session that few members of the House, including Weaver himself, thought the bill had any more than a slim chance of passage in the Senate."[87]

## Senate committee consideration in 1969

Sen. Wayne Popham, Minneapolis Conservative, was chief author in the Senate. He achieved political and geographic balance with his choices of co-authors, Sen. Nicholas Coleman, St. Paul DFLer and Senate minority leader, and Sen. Rollin Glewwe, South St. Paul Conservative.

Albert: "Popham was a leading member of a group of Conservatives which came to be known informally as the 'Young Turks.' They were more liberal-minded and far more active in Republican Party affairs than was the right-leaning 'old guard' which dominated the Conservative caucus . . ."[88]

The House-passed bill was sent to the Senate on May 17, 11 days before scheduled adjournment.[89]

Albert: "It received cursory attention during a May 22 meeting of the Tax Committee. Popham explained the bill, and Majority Leader Stanley Holmquist spoke briefly in favor . . . The committee resolved to discuss the proposal again on the following day, but a strange series of events prevented that committee meeting from taking place."[90]

In his book *Thinking Out the How* Kolderie described the events: "In the Senate, coming down to the final day, the bill was stuck in committee. The Tax Committee, chaired by Sen. Donald Wright, had one last hearing. Wright called around the business community, looking for someone to testify in opposition. Fred Cady from Honeywell, who was on the Citizens League Board in 1969, said no. John Barker, from General Mills, said no. Wright canceled the hearing."[91]

Albert: "Wright . . . found a perfect excuse on the morning of the planned hearing. Members of the Minneapolis Tenants Union, angered by the Legislature's 'failure to act' on social legislation and welfare programs, decided to hold a demonstration in the Senate Chamber. The body used a little-known power and voted to declare an exceptional 'state of urgency' to exist, a move which set aside all rules and normal procedures. Though the disturbance was under control in a few minutes' time, Wright used the state of urgency as a rationale for canceling the hearing."[92]

Republican Harold LeVander, governor in 1969 but who did run for re-election in 1970, was supportive of Weaver's effort. LeVander was quoted in the *Citizens League News* as being "intrigued" with the bill.[93]

# Non-property taxes for local government strongly enters discussion between legislative sessions in 1969 and 1971

A significant advantage of tax-base sharing—that it dealt with reducing differences in capacity to raise revenue but did not raise revenue itself—was to some extent a negative feature for some local governments. Local governments' first priority was non-property revenue to reduce their reliance on the property tax. That issue became prominent between the 1969 and 1971 Legislatures.

In 1969-1971 the Minnesota Legislature still met in regular session only in the odd-numbered year. Thus following the 1969 session formal action on any legislation would need to wait until 1971.

Proposals for non-property revenues emerged from many sources in 1969-1970: the Metropolitan Council, the Weaver subcommittee, the Metro Section of the League of Municipalities, the chambers of commerce, the League of Women Voters, the Citizens League, and others.

## Metropolitan Council

The Metropolitan Council with a new fiscal division staff headed by Allen Muglia began work on developing a larger proposal for providing local government with new non-property revenues.

Albert: " . . . the Metropolitan Council, elated over its success in obtaining legislative passage of a comprehensive sewer bill in the 1969 session, vowed to devote its efforts during the 1969-1970 interim to problems of metropolitan finance . . . Council chairman James L. Hetland, Jr., who also was an active Citizens League member, vocalized the Council's chief concern: that successful implementation of its development authority would be impossible within the existing local fiscal system.

" . . . by November (1970), staff recommendations to the Council, calling for the distribution of new, non-property tax resources according to a 'percentage equalization' plan keyed to relative ability-to-pay, had been promulgated. The Council accepted these proposals just before year's end and issued its own lengthy analysis of the fiscal disparities problem in March 1971. Bills embodying the Council's disparities approach were not introduced until April 8, late in the 1971 legislative session."[94]

## Weaver subcommittee

The Weaver subcommittee reported its interim recommendations in December 1970.

Albert: "First, the general outline of a two-pronged solution for fiscal disparities was suggested: 'greater equalization of the base of financing for all units of local government and school districts' was to be combined with additional revenue from non-property sources . . . Second, the committee stipulated that 'all formulas used to determine disparity or amount of aid should reflect as far as possible personal and community ability to pay and impact of providing services based on need.' Use of tax effort, relative wealth, and pupil unit measures was proposed. Finally, spending limits on municipalities and school districts were said to be necessary to prevent those governmental units from spending any 'windfall' gains which might accrue from increased local aid . . ."[95]

"While the report does not tout the League-Weaver sharing plan as a total panacea—indeed, at one point it says that the plan 'would not solve the problems of providing immediate financial aid to local government,' but should be accompanied by new tax sources—it does treat it quite favorably, especially by contrast . . . The base sharing plan is a central element of each of the combinations of proposals discussed in the report; in a discussion which foreshadows Senate consideration of the League-Weaver plan, the report at one point discusses the possibility of combining the base sharing plan with the Metropolitan Council's formula-based proposal."[96]

## Tax-base sharing in the Minnesota House in the 1971 regular session

Weaver again introduced his tax-base sharing bill, with Sabo and Albertson as co-authors, plus Robert North, St. Paul DFLer, and Howard Knutson, Conservative, from Burnsville. O'Neill and Frenzel, 1969 co-authors, no longer were in the House. O'Neill was elected to the state Senate in 1970 and Frenzel was elected to Congress, where he served through 1990 (including service as a prominent member of the House Ways and Means Committee).

Albert: "Weaver had been most anxious to obtain Knutson's support, and had actively pursued it; Weaver was well aware that Knutson's district included several of the southern suburbs likely to be most violently opposed to the base sharing plan, and hoped to head off some opposition by co-opting the Burnsville representative."[97]

As it had in 1969 the bill moved quickly through the House, approved 90-42 on March 31. A motion by Rep. Raymond Pavlak, South St. Paul DFLer, to refer the bill to the Tax Committee was defeated 75-15. "Nine of the 18 Twin Cities-area opponents of the bill in yesterday's vote were from Minneapolis and St. Paul," the *Minneapolis Star* reported.[98]

Orfield in *Metropolitics* said the vote involved a coalition of poorer suburbs, outstate legislators, and some central city legislators against richer suburbs and other outstate legislators.[99]

Albert: "Two days of House debate on the bill resulted in only one change: properties pledged under the aegis of housing and redevelopment authorities (HRAs) were exempted from sharing, a move designed to stave off increasing criticism of the bill's potentially adverse effects on HRA redevelopment plans."[100]

## Attaching the Metropolitan Council proposal to the Senate's bill on tax-base sharing

As in 1969 Popham was the Senate author, with Coleman and Glewwe, co-authors. Popham held off on trying to move the bill until the House acted. During this time Metropolitan Council strategies shifted.

Albert: "It had become increasingly clear to the Metropolitan Council staffers managing the Council's new disparities proposal that they were getting nowhere.

"Obviously, League-Weaver had acquired a momentum which was difficult to ignore. Moreover, this momentum had been forged at the cost of setting aside the new-revenue-source proposals . . . It was apparent that some sort of accommodation with the proponents of the League-Weaver bill would be necessary to salvage any part of the Council's proposal."[101]

Albert: "Council representatives approached Popham with their proposal for merging the two bills, and found a receptive ear. Neither Popham nor Weaver had misgivings about the merger; both were eager to appease the opposition, even if friendly, in order to broaden their base of support."[102]

The formula for distribution of shared tax base was changed from straight per capita to include a measure of fiscal capacity—whether a community was above or below average in total tax base. A new section was added to the bill creating a municipal equity account.

Albert: "One would have expected the addition of a major new element, in the form of the Municipal Equity Account, to raise some eyebrows. Yet it did not, principally because no one took it seriously . . . These proposals were incorporated into the League-Weaver bill through a group of amendments formally adopted on April 17."[103] The Municipal Equity Account was not then and never was funded. Ultimately the authorizing language for the account was deleted from the statute.

The Senate bill was referred to the Committee on Metropolitan and Urban Affairs. Albert reports that after a string of positive testimony, opponents led by Sen. Jerome Blatz, now chair of the Tax Committee, were sufficiently effective attacking the mechanics of the bill that Sen. Harmon Ogdahl, chair of the Senate Urban Affairs Committee, on Popham's suggestion named a subcommittee to review the issue. Sen. William McCutcheon, St. Paul, was named chair. Other members were Sen. Stanley Thorup of Blaine, Sen. William G. Kirchner, Richfield, Popham, and Ogdahl himself.

Albert: " . . . he (Ogdahl) knew that with three central-city subcommittee members, he could get a favorable report . . . Ogdahl's suspicions about the leanings of his appointed five proved correct; the subcommittee voted 3-2 to report the bill favorably . . . [104]

"Opponents made a last attempt to discredit the bill on mechanical grounds. Dakota County Administrator W. C. 'Andy' Anderson produced a resolution, signed by the auditors of all seven metropolitan counties, which charged that the 'orderly continued administration of the property tax system' was threatened by the base sharing bill, and urged that any future consideration of such measures 'be conducted using individuals who understand all processes involved'—i.e., the auditors."[105]

The bill was sent to the full Senate on a voice vote of the full committee with Blatz and Thorup dissenting.[106] During committee discussion Blatz continued his claim that the bill "cannot be understood. I defy anyone to say he understands this bill." According to the *Star Tribune* account, Wallace Dahl, research director for the State Tax Department, supported Blatz' concern.

## Late-session controversy

As a constitutionally-established requirement for legislative adjournment approached in late May 1971, a host of bills remained on the agenda, including tax-base sharing and major proposals for school aids and municipal aids, over which DFL Gov. Wendell Anderson and Republican legislators were at odds. Also tax-base sharing authors were seeking to diffuse a problem in South St. Paul, which was in the district of Sen. Rollin Glewwe, co-author on the tax-base sharing bill.

Albert: "Representatives of South St. Paul, an inner-ring stockyard center facing high unemployment and a markedly diminished tax base in the aftermath of the folding of one of its largest employers, raised strong objections to the bill in fear that it would hamper their recovery efforts . . . Their (proponents' of the bill) solution, adopted on the Senate floor on May 22, was a classic example of accommodative politics: all localities declared 'economically distressed areas' were to be exempted from contribution of base. On the surface, it sounded reasonable; in reality, it applied only to South St. Paul."[107]

## Last-minute rescue in the Senate

In the last day of the regular session tax-base sharing was kept alive to be considered in a special session, perhaps aided unwittingly by Blatz, who could have prevented passage.

Albert: "Popham was anxious to move to a vote on the bill, since Stanley Holmquist, majority leader and chairman of the Rules Committee had announced that only bills which had been acted upon by both houses would be considered in the upcoming extra session . . . Blatz agreed to drop his ideas of filibustering and allow a vote, on the condition that it would be understood that such a vote was taken only for the purpose of allowing extra session consideration of the measure. Since the Senate version differed from that passed by the House, this parliamentary trick would work only so long as no conference committee was formed. Assured that that would be the case, Blatz relented, the bill passed on an unrecorded vote, and in effect died only hours later, at the session's end."[108]

In a footnote (no. 66, chapter 3) to his thesis, Albert writes of an interview he had with Blatz on July 19, 1978.

Albert—" . . ."Blatz passed up a golden opportunity to block the bill by failing to push for its referral to the Tax Committee, which he chaired. He recalls that he did not make such an effort because it would have been so 'blatant;' everyone knew he was after the bill. In retrospect, he sees this as a strategic error; he is convinced that he 'could've beaten it' in his own committee."

Blatz was advocating for a value-added tax at the same time. Possibly he thought his avoiding extreme measures to kill tax-base sharing might help garner votes for a value-added tax. Perhaps he chose not to abuse his power against a bill advocated by his friend, Weaver. Whatever his reasons, the bill would not likely have passed had Blatz insisted that the bill be referred to his committee.

## Special session drama in the Senate

Albert: "The extra legislative session convened on May 25; Popham immediately reintroduced the League-Weaver-Council bill in its final, amended form. Like all bills in the extra session, it was referred to the Rules Committee, which received it on May 26 and reported it out the next day with a 'special order to be heard immediately'. This parliamentary device was not as drastic as it may sound; of the 225 bills considered by the committee during the extra session, 55 were given similar 'special orders' . . . The committee's action on the fiscal disparities bill, moreover, was no surprise; committee chairman Holmquist had supported the legislation for some time, and Ogdahl and Popham sat on the committee."[109]

Until this point, through the 1969 and 1971 sessions, the full Senate had never taken a recorded vote on tax-base sharing.

"On June 1, Holmquist (in his role of majority leader) moved the bill . . . to the status of a 'special order to be heard immediately,' thus bringing the bill to a final vote. Popham, relieved to finally reach the point of decision on the 'most complicated thing he ever handled' in the Legislature, was fairly confident of victory; he expected 37 or 38 affirmative votes. He was overly optimistic; on the roll call, he received the 34-vote majority which Senate rules required for passage and nothing more, producing a final tally of 34-31."[110]

## Special session drama in the House

Albert: "By this time the Senate bill looked quite different from the bill the House had originally passed on March 31 . . . Weaver, Sabo and the rest of the bill's proponents, however, were petrified at the thought of sending the bill back to the Senate through a conference committee. They had not had votes to spare on the June 1 Senate vote; to give their opponents another shot would have been suicide. Consequently, they substituted the Senate version for the version previously approved by the House . . . determined to pass the Senate version as it stood . . ."[111]

"When floor debate on the bill finally commenced on July 2, suburban opponents, led by Rep. Joseph Graw (C-Bloomington), strongly criticized the bill and introduced a series of amendments designed to kill it, but to no avail . . . Amidst widespread speculation that House approval was now a foregone conclusion, a final vote was set for July 9 or 12."[112]

But it turned out that all would not be clear sailing. Rep. Martin Sabo, House minority leader and a co-author of Weaver's bill, threatened that he and other DFLers would not support Weaver "because of an 'indefinable frustration' over actions of the House Conservatives on taxes and the refusal of the Conservative leadership to permit some other bills to reach the House floor . . . A governor's aide said it would be a 'serious mistake' for Weaver to permit a final vote on the bill before 'DFLers have cooled down.'"[113]

Albert: "A shaken Weaver put off a final vote until later in the week; he was well aware that, even if every House Conservative supported him, he would still need eleven DFL votes to gain passage."[114]

Weaver's cause was helped by a *Minneapolis Tribune* editorial that said, "It will be unfortunate, in our opinion, if the DFL carries out this threat. The bill is far too important to be killed on a partisan basis or . . . out of liberal 'frustration' over actions of the House Conservatives. Such an action would be illogical, since fiscal disparities is not a partisan plan . . . Nor would killing the bill be in the DFL's self-interest, for the 'have-not' parts of the metropolitan area tend, in general, to lean some-what more toward Democrats than to Republicans."[115]

Albert: "Apparently, the advice was taken. DFLers such as Tom Berg of Minneapolis and E. W. Quirin of Rochester asked fellow liberals' support during the final floor debate, and 26 joined a sold block of 57 Conservatives in propelling the bill to a 83-39 victory on July 15. Amidst editorialized boasts of 'an unprecedented step by a state to deal with urban fiscal problems', Gov. Anderson signed the bill into law on July 23."[116]

During debate on the House floor Graw predicted the plan would mark the "beginning of the erosion of the local tax base.[117] He also warned that the measure would pose virtually insurmountable administrative problems." Rep. Robert Pavlak, St. Paul Conservative, was opposed and unsuccessfully attempted to obtain an exclusion for developments under-taken by the St. Paul Port Authority, and Rep. John Salchert, Minneapo-lis DFLer, was opposed and unsuccessfully sought a one-year exemption for Minneapolis.

"Meanwhile, considerable opposition came from outstate DFLers who warned that the plan might eventually be extended to the entire state—with adverse consequences," the *Tribune* reported.

## Analysis of final votes in House and Senate

Albert explains the vote by metro area Senators as "strikingly well-explained in terms of self-interest". He noted unanimous support from the

15 central city Senators, but three-fourths of suburban Senators voted no. "Of the four suburban Senators who voted affirmatively, one was a co-author of the bill; another, while representing a number of well-to-do suburbs, had significant business interests in the downtown area."[118]

Albert: "The Senate vote hinged, then, on the votes of the thirty-four outstate Senators. Unlike their House counterparts' later vote, which was sharply divided along partisan lines . . . their vote is best explained in terms of ideology. Outstate negative votes were anchored in a 'hard core of conservative opposition,' variously estimated at seven to ten in number, which 'never, under any conditions' would have supported the bill . . . Their effectiveness was tempered to some extent by the influence of the majority and minority leaders in the Senate (Holmquist and Coleman, respectively), both strong supporters of the bill. Coleman was particularly important in 'bringing along' several outstate DFLers."[119]

According to Albert, the House vote was significantly partisan, with 86 percent of House Conservatives voting yes, compared to 46 percent of DFLers. "To some extent, this divergence is the expression of a conservatism which typified many of these 'second generation' rural DFLers, who tended to be more conservative than their predecessors."[120]

Albert: "The most notable divergence between the two houses' voting patterns, however, is seen in the votes of suburban legislators. In the Senate suburban opposition generally followed lines of self-interest. In the House, however, two-thirds of the suburban representatives supported the base sharing measure. While suburban Conservatives' support was stronger than that of their DFL counterparts, even the suburban DFLers gave base sharing a slight majority—six of eleven voted for the measure. To some extent, this Conservative support stems from Weaver's efforts; as a talented, well-respected suburban Conservative, his influence was substantial. But the principal explanation must lie in a fundamental denial of self-interested voting . . ."[121]

## The mechanics of tax-base sharing

Tax-base sharing is relatively easy to express: all municipalities are guaranteed a share of the growth in commercial-industrial property wherever in the area that growth is physically located. That's sufficient for some readers. Others may rely on detailed step-by-step examples in official governmental documents, such as a 2020 House Research report.[122]

However, some readers won't bother to consult a government document, and for them a one-sentence description leaves too many questions unanswered. So what follows is an effort at a middle-of-the-road explanation, with a caveat. It's not *exactly* how the law is written. As initially enacted, the law included procedures that made it difficult for annual tax statements to be mailed on time. So five years later the Legislature enacted a change that eased time pressures on county tax administrators. The change doesn't affect the impact of the law but makes it more difficult to explain. Here's a "pure" version, before the administrative change:

In tax-base sharing 40 percent of growth in commercial-industrial (C/I) assessed value since 1971 is (mathematically) removed from each municipality's local tax base and placed in a virtual entity known as the **areawide tax base**. This removal from the local tax base is not conducted property-by-property, but rather on an aggregate basis for the municipality. So in each municipality a **contribution percentage** is determined equal to the total amount of tax base removed divided by the municipality's total (commercial-industrial) tax base. Currently, the contribution percentage of the average municipality is about 35 percent. The percentage varies among municipalities because it represents 40 percent of the municipality's post-1971 C/I value growth divided by its current C/I value.

The areawide tax base is distributed back to municipalities on the basis of population, adjusted for the municipality's per capita tax base relative to that of other municipalities. Every municipality contributes and every municipality shares, with some municipalities receiving more than they contributed and some, less. Overlapping taxing districts (counties, school districts and special taxing districts) are assigned proportionate shares of the areawide tax base contributions and distributions of the municipalities located wholly or partly within their borders.

The areawide tax base in total may not be levied-on by any municipality. Each municipality is authorized to impose a dollar levy on its assigned share of the areawide tax base, as if that share were actual property within its borders.

After tax-base sharing is applied, each taxing jurisdiction's resulting tax base is composed of the assessed value of (a) all residential property, (b) the local portion of all C/I property, and (c) the jurisdiction's share of the areawide tax base. The total levy of each jurisdiction is then divided proportionately between (a) its local tax base (residential property plus local portion of C/I property) and (b) its share of the areawide tax base. The levy thus allocated to the local base is then divided by that base, and the resulting local tax rate is applied to each parcel of local value to calculate the local tax on that parcel. The total of the levies of all jurisdictions allocated to the areawide base is similarly divided by that base, the resulting areawide tax rate is applied to the areawide portion of each C/I parcel in the metro area, and the resulting taxes are distributed to the levying jurisdictions. The application of a uniform areawide tax rate on a portion of all C/I property in the area has the effect of narrowing property tax differences among municipalities on similarly-valued property.

In actual operation, the portion of a jurisdiction's levy allocated to the areawide tax base is determined by applying its prior year local tax rate to its current year share of the areawide tax base, and the portion allocated to its local tax base is determined by subtracting its resulting areawide levy from its total levy.

## Tax-base sharing was a significant, but smaller, part of famous "Minnesota Miracle"

In September 1970 the Citizens League issued another report on local government finance, this one with a much broader coverage and greater impact in that immediate time frame.[123] The report became the focus of a campaign for governor between DFLer Wendell R. Anderson and Republican Douglas Head. The candidates were featured at the 1970 Citizens League annual meeting at the Saint Paul Hotel, with Anderson, who ultimately was elected, supporting the report and Head, opposing it.[124]

The League's recommendation for full state support of operating budgets of schools up to the median per pupil cost across the state was endorsed by Anderson and attracted the most controversy. Subsequently, Rep. Martin Sabo, a key architect of the Legislative package, wisely saw that the effect of 100 percent state support could be accomplished technically, without having the state pay 100 percent directly to the schools. A state-mandated local property tax levy, uniform across all school districts, equalized for differences in assessment practices, could be regarded as part of state-funding even though it were a local levy. The levy was uniform across all school districts.

The 1971 Legislature ended up enacting " . . . the outstanding fiscal case study of the year," said the Advisory Commission on Intergovernmental Relations (ACIR), Washington, D. C.[125] The ACIR headlined this part of the annual report "The Minnesota Miracle", a phrase that has been used over and over in years since as shorthand for Minnesota's fiscal-related actions in 1971 as well as to describe non-fiscal-related achievements, such as a game-winning touchdown for the Minnesota Vikings.[126]

"By assuming a dominant role in state-local fiscal policymaking, they (Minnesota legislators) intended to reduce the fiscal disparities among school districts, strengthen the general fiscal position of municipalities and counties and ease the burden of property taxes on home owners and business firms. In the process, they made Minnesota a model for other states to follow," the ACIR said.[127]

The fiscal-related actions followed very closely the recommendations of the Citizens League in its 1970 report. The League summarized the legislative actions:[128]

A comprehensive revision of the school aid formula, designed to assure equality of opportunity for students throughout the state, regardless of their socio-economic background or the wealth of the school districts where they live.

A comprehensive revision of the formulas for distribution of state aid to municipalities, villages, townships and counties . . . and on providing funds for those units of government most in need of additional financing.

A large infusion of state non-property revenues to local government accompanied by mandatory reductions in local property tax levies and by strict limits on local property taxes . . .

A prohibition against further sales or income taxes being levied by any local government.

A sharing of 40 percent of the future growth in commercial-industrial property tax base among all units of government in the seven-county Twin Cities area.

A partial shift in financing county highways from the property tax to a wheelage tax, accompanied by an authority for the Metropolitan Transit Commission to levy a limited property tax . . .

## Tax-base sharing is not a way to give more money to hard-pressed municipalities

Minnesota's 1971 actions on state-local tax and finance resulted in widespread interest from other states. Interest was particularly high among hard-pressed central cities in other metropolitan areas. Minnesota's scheme was seen as a way for such municipalities to tap suburbia's wealth. In actuality had tax-base sharing in Minnesota been characterized or designed in such a way, it never would have passed.

First, as its framers appreciated—and as others inside and outside Minnesota gradually came to realize—tax-base sharing didn't raise new revenue for hard-pressed local governments to spend, whether central city, suburban or rural. Instead it slightly modified the burden that taxpayers assume when local governments impose (or "levy" as the professionals say) local property taxes. Taxpayers with an abundance of commercial-industrial growth in coming years would be paying a bit more than they otherwise would, and taxpayers in communities with less growth wouldn't be quite as heavily burdened.

Of course, no one knew for certain in 1971 where future growth would take place. Nevertheless, it would not have required a Ph.D. from the University of Minnesota to anticipate that future commercial-industrial growth was most likely to favor southwest suburbs, which already had a head start. In the central cities St. Paul figured to gain. Minneapolis, too, but that was a bit less certain. Aside from who wins and who loses, the metro area now had unity it never had before. The newly-formed Metropolitan Council law had assembled the 190-plus pieces (municipalities and townships) of the seven-county metro puzzle, and, as chief author Charles R. Weaver said, tax-base sharing provided the glue that would hold the pieces of the puzzle together.

## Differences in taxes on C/I property are narrowed

Because of tax-base sharing, C/I properties pay neither the highest, nor the lowest rates in the region. Property tax rates on C/I property throughout the metro area as of the year 2020 are the same for about 35 percent of the value of each C/I parcel, with the rate being a weighted average of all local property tax rates in the seven-county metro area. The remaining 65 percent of value of each parcel pays the local rate. There's no tax haven in the metro area for C/I property and no location where such property would pay extraordinarily higher rates.

If all communities in the metro area by some quirk were to receive back from the tax-base sharing pool exactly what they had contributed, would there be any change in property taxes? Absolutely. The portion of C/I property in each community that is contributed to the tax-base sharing pool will be taxed at a rate that is the weighted average of all local property tax rates in the metro area. The remaining portion of each parcel of C/I property bears the local property tax rate. That relationship holds whether the community gains, loses, or breaks even on shared tax-base.

## The "losers" are still the "winners"; the" winners" are still the "losers"

Everyone wins, because everyone has a stake in, and a guaranteed share of, future commercial-industrial growth in the seven-county metro area, permanently, irrespective of where in the metro area that growth happens to occur.

It is as if everyone has a tax-base insurance policy. The benefit of the policy: a guaranteed share of metro area growth, even if that growth occurs outside your borders. The premium in the policy: you yield some of the growth occurring within your borders to the rest of the region. Over time, just as in regular insurance, the benefit will exceed the premium, or vice versa.

In a discussion of the fact that Minneapolis in 1984 would, for the first time, be a net contributor to the tax-base sharing pool, a *Minneapolis Star and Tribune* editorial noted that Minneapolis became a net contributor "only because Minneapolis's commercial-industrial growth is finally catching up with, even surpassing, the regional pace—which is good news indeed."[129]

A claim that a community is either a winner or loser, needs to be very cautiously stated. A city might be a net contributor in tax base but the county and school district in which the city is located might be net gainers, meaning that overall its taxpayers are gaining, even though their community seems to be a net contributor. The opposite also can be true. A city might be a net gainer, but its county and school district might be net contributors, so its taxpayers would be losing. In the early 1980s at least one suburb mistakenly included itself in a "Losers Group", overlooking the fact that even though the suburb was a net contributor, its school district and county were net gainers.

## Newcomers to a metro area city now bring more tax base with them

Before tax-base sharing, municipalities often were concerned whether they could raise sufficient tax revenue to cover expenses of the services new residents imposed—on schools, on police, fire and other services. But that fear is diminished under tax-base sharing. Each city's share of the metropolitan tax-base sharing pool is related to the city's population. More people, more C/I tax base.

## Big decision 1: what specific tax base should be pooled

In deciding the amount of tax base to be contributed to the metropolitan pool, the Legislature didn't quarrel much with the Citizens League proposal that was incorporated in Charles R. Weaver's bill—that only future growth would be shared; that only growth in commercial-industrial value would be shared. The Citizens League suggested 50 percent of commercial-industrial would remain local, and 50 percent shared. The

Legislature changed that provision to 60 percent, local, and 40 percent, shared.

A major effort led by Rep. Myron Orfield to include a portion of homestead value passed the 1995 Legislature but was vetoed by Gov. Arne Carlson.

A clarifying question concerning how shared growth is determined doesn't occur to everyone, but is significant in understanding details. The entire C/I valuation in the municipality in the current year is compared to the C/I valuation in 1971. Forty percent of the growth since 1971 is excluded from the local tax base. That exclusion is taken proportionately from every parcel of C/I value, irrespective of whether a parcel experienced growth. Consequently, the local tax rate and areawide tax rate apply to the same percentages of every C/I parcel within the same municipality.

## Big decision 2: how the pooled tax base should be shared

The League proposed, and the Legislature provided in law, that all the pooled tax base would be returned to the local jurisdictions from which the tax base came. None of the value would be held at the areawide level for other purposes, although some proposals to that end have been advanced in subsequent years.

The League recommended straight per capita distribution: a community's percentage of the seven-county population would be its share of the metropolitan pool. Given that the distribution in tax-base sharing affects all local government units, including school districts and counties as well as municipalities, per capita seemed a practical option across such units. The League considered that "fine-tuning" formulas, such as including individual income, disadvantaged children, and age of housing are more appropriate to include when distributing revenue, not tax base. The Legislature ended up modifying the League's per capita recommendation by enacting a recommendation from the Metropolitan Council to give a higher-than-per-capita distribution to municipalities below average in total tax base per capita and a lower distribution to municipalities above average.

Factors of "need" and "ability to pay" were recommended on aid to school districts and municipalities in other sections of the League's reports on local government finance and enacted into law by the Minnesota Legislature in 1971. So when tax-base sharing is reviewed in the context of the entire package of state-local fiscal relationships in 1971, it is clear that "need" and "ability to pay" were an integral part

## Near death several times, but healthy today

Despite the fact that tax-base sharing has been widely acclaimed since its approval in 1971, its survival was highly questionable, particularly in the early years.

In retrospect, it seems almost unbelievable that the idea ever got proposed and enacted, let alone that it survived for all these years. Time and again, once an obstacle was addressed and overcome, dramatically another appeared.

If the originator of tax-base sharing had kept the idea to himself and not shared it late in 1968 with the Citizens League committee, it's uncertain whether it ever would have seen the light of day.

If a Citizens League subcommittee member early in 1969 had turned a 4-4 vote to 3-5, the full Citizens League committee might never have endorsed the concept.

If in 1969 a respected lawyer—whose opinions on bond issues were taken as gospel, and who himself had been on the losing side in the Citizens League committee—had not indicated in a letter that tax-base sharing would work mechanically, even though he opposed the idea, tax-base sharing assuredly would have died.

If the chair of the Minnesota Senate Tax Committee in the 1971 regular session had asked that the bill be referred to his committee, it never would have been sent to the floor.

If one member of a bare majority in the 1971 special session Minnesota Senate had decided to vote no, tax base sharing would not have passed the Legislature.

If one member of a bare majority in the Minnesota Supreme Court had decided to vote no, the decision of the District Court declaring tax-base sharing unconstitutional would not have been reversed.

If a way had not been found in 1979 to make tax-base sharing work in tax-increment districts, its significance would have been substantially reduced.

Had a sharing exemption been granted in 1985 to the site of the Mall of America, the likelihood of more such exemptions would have increased, substantially diluting the impact of tax-base sharing.

## Would urban development be better off without a property tax?

The property tax has plenty of critics.[130] Theoretically, if local units of government didn't levy property taxes locally and instead received their revenues as grants from state or federal governments, local taxes would be unrelated to whether C/I property were located in one municipality or another. But local governments would lose their independence and be fully at the mercy of higher levels of government.

As long as municipalities finance a significant portion of their budgets from locally-raised revenues—whether sales, income, or property taxes or other sources—their governing bodies will always consider local revenue implications of their land use decisions. If they rely less on local property taxes and more on local sales and income taxes, as is the case in some parts of the nation, local revenue implications of those sources are every bit as important as property taxes. The fiscal implications of metropolitanism are present in all locally controlled revenue sources.

Whether a tax is regressive (with the rate highest at lower incomes), proportional (with the rate same for all incomes), or progressive (with the rate lowest at lower incomes), depends on how the tax is structured. Sales, income and property taxes are not inherently regressive, proportional or progressive; it all depends upon how they are designed.

# CHAPTER 4

## Implementing tax-base sharing: County cooperation was essential

### The big task facing employees in the seven county assessors' and auditors' offices

Citizens League leaders knew full well that integrating tax-base sharing into an already very complex Minnesota property tax system would not be easy. But the employees in the seven metro counties and the State Department of Revenue exceeded all expectations in fulfilling their responsibilities under the law, irrespective of how they might have felt personally.

Citizens League leaders recognized tax-base sharing would face three major tests: (1) the policy test, which legislators fulfilled, (2) the judicial test, which the Minnesota Supreme Court fulfilled, and (3) the administrative test, getting the program implemented by county officials, which meant assembling the data from the seven counties, making the calculations and sending out the property tax statements.

County assessors and auditors in the seven-county metro area always had a long history of coordinating with one another when figuring out property taxes because of the need to determine tax bills for jurisdictions that were located partly in one county and partly in another, such as St.

Anthony, in both Hennepin and Ramsey Counties. But the fiscal dispari-ties law presented unprecedented challenges. Now all seven counties had to work together. Either they all got their work done or none of them did.

A good amount of insight into the administrative work comes from Karen Baker, now retired, who spent her career first in the Minnesota Department of Revenue, then in Anoka County, and then in the Minne-sota Legislature in the non-partisan House Research office. Baker distinctly recalls that county employees from day one were committed to making tax-base sharing work. Untold meetings among the counties were necessary, plus unparalleled cooperation, because no county could send out its tax statements to property owners unless all seven counties had duly fulfilled their responsibilities. It wasn't easy, Baker recalls, because some counties lagged behind others.

For counties to carry out their responsibilities under the law, the day-to-day job of implementation lay with the hard-working lower-level employees, not so much the directly elected county boards. One of them was Gloria Pinke, who served in the assessor's office in Dakota County from 1969 to 2015. In an interview in March 2020, Pinke noted she already was five years retired but misses the work greatly. She recalls the major efforts she and others in the office went through to assemble the 1971 base values, from which tax-base sharing growth was calculated. She recalls innumerable meetings with her counterparts from the other metro-politan area counties.

An illustration of the readiness of administrative officials to carry out requirements of the law: Arthur Roemer, state commissioner of revenue, on the very day (September 13, 1974) the Supreme Court announced its favorable decision, announced guidelines would be distributed in two weeks.[131] Charles Lefebvre, Anoka County auditor also serving as admin-istrative auditor, that same day said he'd be calling a meeting of the metro-politan auditors and attorneys the following week to discuss how to proceed.[132]

The real mark of county employees' diligence was that on January 17, 1975, Lefebrve released to the public the amounts of tax base contributed and received for all municipalities and townships in the metropolitan area, thereby revealing winners and losers for the first year of implementation.[133] Baker speculates that even before the Supreme Court announced its decision the counties were preparing themselves in case the law were found constitutional.

Tax-base sharing as enacted in 1971 had the effect of requiring county officials to cram more work, faster, into a short time to get the correct information distributed to taxing units for setting their levies. The Legislature in 1976 gave counties more breathing room by providing that the "fiscal disparities contribution and distribution values and tax rates would be based on data from the previous year," according to House Research.[134] For persons interested in the impact of the one-year lag, House Research illustrates the administrative procedures and calculations for a hypothetical municipality both with and without the lag.

Early on Citizens League leaders had been well aware of burdens that would be imposed on county offices. It didn't hurt that county officials had received minutes throughout the work of the Citizens League Fiscal Disparities Committee and could have kept themselves abreast. In an effort to ease people's minds about the complexity and to clearly explain what needed to be done, Citizens League memos were prepared in September 1971, after legislative approval but before a court case delayed implementation, that outlined details, with suggested step-by-step illustrations, of the administrative auditor's and county auditors' new responsibilities.[135]

# CHAPTER 5

## Legitimizing tax-base sharing: Three big lawsuits

## The constitutional question might have been tax-base sharing's biggest hurdle

The question of constitutionality of tax-base sharing lies in the manner the tax burden falls on C/I property. Within any taxing district—say, city, township, school district, county, watershed district or similar entity—property taxpayers are constitutionally guaranteed equal protection under the laws. Thus for an equivalent value of property the rate needs to be same no matter where in the taxing district the property happens to be located.

Under tax-base sharing a uniform metropolitan tax rate is imposed on all shared C/I property, no matter where located. Thus, one may contend that C/I property thereby is assured equal protection under the laws. Moreover, as its promoters have stressed repeatedly, an automatic effect of tax-base sharing is to narrow differences in total property taxes on C/I property throughout the region. Consequently, no C/I property is taxed inordinately high or low, no matter where the property is located in the metro area.

The uniform tax rate applies to 40 percent of the net growth in C/I value since the base year 1971. As that year recedes further into the past the actual percentage of shared C/I value across the seven-county metro area is gradually approaching 40 percent for all C/I properties. In 2020, for instance, the aggregate percentage that shared C/I property bears to the total C/I property in the seven-county area is 35.0 percent.

But, while the portion of a given C/I parcel that bears the uniform metro tax rate is the same within a given city, the portion differs from one city to the next. A larger portion of the value of a given parcel will bear the metro rate in a city where more of its C/I growth has occurred since 1971, in comparison with a city where less of its growth has occurred since then. Even though those differences are not large—and become ever smaller as time goes by—mathematically they still are present. And, of course, the constitutional challenges were brought in the courts in the early years of tax-base sharing, when the differences were much greater than now.

The constitutional question for owners of residential property is a bit different. No tax-base sharing occurs and no uniform rate is applied to any portion of residential value. But residential rates are higher or lower depending upon the value of C/I property in the tax base, including the city's assigned portion of the tax-base sharing pool. Residential property tax rates always have differed depending upon how much C/I property is located within the city limits. But a question of equal protection under the laws can occur when residential property owners contend their taxes are increased because a portion of their C/I value is being transferred elsewhere unfairly.

## Burnsville challenges tax-base sharing in District Court

In 1972, before tax-base sharing could actually be implemented, the village of Burnsville challenged its constitutionality in Dakota County District Court.[136] Citizens Leaguers and other supporters undoubtedly were deeply troubled about the future of their creative initiative. No one could have anticipated that not until 1998 would court challenges end. But it probably was for the best that the initial challenge occurred before sharing took place, rather than having the program start and be subjected to later interruption.

Burnsville, a Dakota County suburb immediately south of the Minnesota River, in 1972 was a comparatively new urbanizing community, having changed from a township to a village nine years earlier. The population of the village was growing rapidly, from 2,716 in 1960 to 19,940 in 1970. It had a strong tax base, anchored by the Northern States Power Co. Black Dog plant, that would not be subject to sharing. Its major shopping center would not be built for five more years.

Interestingly, three persons active in promoting tax-base sharing were Burnsville residents. F. Warren Preeshl, who originated the concept of tax-base sharing in the Citizens League, was a resident and a member of the Burnsville School Board. Then State-Rep. Howard Knutson of Burnsville (later elected a State Senator) was an author of Rep. Charles R. Weaver's tax-base sharing bill, although after the law was found constitutional Knutson signed on to a bill to repeal the law. Paul Gilje, research director of the Citizens League and staff for the League committee that recommended tax-base sharing, was a resident.

The city of Bloomington, a larger suburb located immediately north of Burnsville, was reported to be considering a similar suit.[137] but its City Council decided against it.[138] The day before Burnsville filed its suit, the Twin Cities metro area was honored by the National Municipal League as an "All America City". Noting the juxtaposition, the *Minneapolis Tribune* editorialized : "But now, ironically, the Twin Cities area will fully deserve the All-America award only if it turns away from the beggar-thy-neighbor attitudes exemplified by opposition to the fiscal disparities law."[139]

The District Court challenge was heard by Judge Robert J. Breunig. Breunig, later to be chief judge of the First Judicial District (Carver, Dakota, Goodhue, Le Sueur, McLeod, Scott and Sibley Counties), was appointed to the bench in 1964 by Gov. Karl Rolvaag, a DFLer. In 1962 Breunig had represented Rolvaag in a ballot recount in which Rolvaag unseated Republican Gov. Elmer L. Andersen. Breunig retired in 1988.[140]

## District Court invalidates tax-base sharing as unconstitutional

In his January 29, 1973, ruling, Breunig found tax-base sharing violated Minnesota Constitution Article 9, Section 1, which provides that "Taxes shall be uniform upon the same class of subjects . . ."

Breunig wrote that tax-base sharing "fails to pass the test not only of practical and common sense equality but totally fails to pass the test of constitutional uniformity requiring that the burden of a tax must fall equally and impartially upon all persons and properties subject to it."[141]

Property tax rates on equivalent values within a given city, village, town, or school district or other "taxing district" are supposed to be uniform, Breunig said, but under tax-base sharing the rates on C/I are different. "Its (the law's) plan imposes a tax on some districts for the benefit of others. It establishes a non-uniform classification of property within a seven county area since it does not exempt that area from its existing statewide classification," Breunig wrote.

"Why should we foot the bill for Minneapolis and St. Paul to build big facilities downtown and take development away from us?" Patrick McInnis, Burnsville village manager, said following the court's ruling. "They want to jam everything into downtown Minneapolis. It hasn't worked in other cities and it won't work here."[142]

## District Court decision appealed to Minnesota Supreme Court

The state of Minnesota, the Metropolitan Council, and Anoka, Carver and Scott counties appealed the District Court decision to the Minnesota Supreme Court. The Supreme Court heard arguments in the case on September 28, 1973. As reported by the *Minneapolis Star*:[143]

Vance B. Grannis, Sr., and Vance B. Grannis, Jr., attorneys for Burnsville, plaintiff in the suit, said the law makes no mention of a special taxing district, and that it is unconstitutional to collect taxes in one municipality, which might go, for instance, to pay for the mayor's salary in another municipality.

John W. Windhorst, Jr., attorney for the defendants, metropolitan area county auditors and the state treasurer, argued that the law clearly implies that a special taxing district is set up. The metropolitan area as a whole has an interest and benefit in, for example, the construction of a school or development of a park by one unit of government, regardless of location, he said.

The Citizens League (on the state's side) and the city of Bloomington (on Burnsville's side) submitted *amicus curiae*, or "friend of the court" briefs.

The Citizens League brief was prepared by three of a large cadre of young lawyers active in the Citizens League, from Republican Party and DFL Party backgrounds. The three were Allen I. Saeks, of Leonard, Street & Deinard; Greer Lockhart, of Bassford Remele, and Earl F. Colborn, Jr., who had chaired the Citizens League Fiscal Disparities Committee, and was with the Fredrikson, Byron law firm. Highlights of the brief:[144]

> In considering the constitutionality of Chapter 24, this Court should consider the direction given by the United States Supreme Court in Rodriguez, supra, that it is the state legislatures which must find the solutions to the fiscal disparities problems that have plagued the states. The Minnesota Legislature anticipated that direction and has produced a nationally acclaimed piece of legislation. The Act not only re-structures financial incentives so as to improve equally the quality of life for all the citizens of the metropolitan area, but also accomplishes its goal in a manner carefully preserving to local units of government their taxing and spending powers . . .

The Bloomington amicus brief, filed by Robert D. Heacock, Jr., assistant city attorney, emphasized that Bloomington was challenging only the constitutionality of the method used by the new law. "Plaintiffs throughout this case, and the City of Bloomington in its Amicus brief to the District Court, have never disputed either the existence of fiscal disparities nor the propriety of the Legislature in seeking to eliminate or control them," Heacock wrote. The brief's central arguments:[145]

Chapter 24 imposes a tax on some existing taxing jurisdictions for the general benefit of other existing taxing jurisdictions.

No new taxing district is created under Chapter 24.

Chapter 24's method of taxation is unconstitutional because there is no reasonable relationship between the taxes imposed upon a district and the benefits it is to derive from the tax.

If the creation of a new metro-area taxing district by Chapter 24 is assumed, the law fails to establish uniformity in its classification and assessment procedures.

## Supreme Court reverses District Court and upholds constitutionality

The Minnesota Supreme Court reversed the District Court and upheld the constitutionality of tax-base sharing on September 13, 1974.[146] The vote was 4-3, with Justices Oscar Knutson, James C. Otis, Jr., Walter Rogesheske, and Harry MacLaughlin voting in the majority, and Justices Fallon Kelly, C. Donald Peterson and Lawrence Yetka in dissent. Robert Sheran, newly appointed Chief Justice, did not participate in the decision because he became a member of the Court after arguments had taken place. Justices John J. Todd and George M. Scott took no part in the consideration or decision in the case.[147]

In response to a request, Windhorst in June 2020 wrote a summary of the Court's reasoning:

The Minnesota Supreme Court held that the issue presented by the case was whether the governmental units that are net contributors to the area-wide tax base are sufficiently "benefited" by the statute to satisfy the uniformity clause of the Minnesota Constitution ("taxes shall be uniform upon the same class of subjects"). Although the Court acknowledged that some of its prior decisions had interpreted the uniformity clause as precluding the distribution of tax proceeds to subordinate governmental units for the purpose of enabling them to satisfy their own obligations, it held that "it is no longer necessary for units of government providing tax revenue to receive the kind of tangible and specific benefits to which our court has previously referred" to satisfy the uniformity clause. In reaching this conclusion, the Court relied upon the reasoning of the then-recent decision of the U.S. Supreme Court in *San Antonio School District v. Rodriguez*, 411 U.S. 1 (1973), in which the validity of the Texas school finance system was upheld on the ground that state legislatures possess broad discretion in devising tax programs. Following a discussion of the fiscal disparities act in light of these principles, the Court concluded that the interdependence of the governmental units and residents of the metropolitan area justified the metro-wide sharing of tax benefits arising from commercial-industrial property growth.

## Otis writes precedent-setting opinion

Justice Otis, appointed to the Court in 1961 by Gov. Elmer L. Andersen, wrote the majority opinion. Excerpts from Otis' opinion:

Our decision to reverse therefore hinges on what we deem to be a developing concept of the meaning of the word "benefit." It seems to us that the phrase "special benefit" no longer adequately serves the constitutional requirement of uniformity. In a seven-county area which is heavily populated, we are of the opinion that it is no longer necessary for units of government providing tax revenue to receive the kind of tangible and specific benefits to which our court has previously referred in order to satisfy the uniformity clause . . .

The fiscal disparities statute is a bold and imaginative departure from conventional devices for balancing the benefits and burdens of taxation. As we have suggested, we are quick to concede that a strict application of our prior decisions would require us to lean strongly for affirmance. The trial court cannot be faulted for reading those decisions as it did. Nevertheless, we are today dealing with a viable, fluid, transient society where traditional concepts of what confers a tax benefit may be too parochial . . .

We find the arguments of defendants persuasive. Under existing tax practices, in order to improve their fiscal capacity, local units of government vie for commerce and industry to improve the fiscal capacity of its residents without considering the resulting impact on long-range planning and the utilization of their resources. The seven-county metropolitan area, it is pointed out, has a high degree of mobility and political, social, and economic interdependence. There is an increasing use of facilities in one municipality by those who reside or work in a different municipality. The payment of taxes in a metropolitan area may have only slight relationship to the use and enjoyment which residents make of other areas in the district . . .

. . . the benefits conferred on residents of a particular municipality because of the location of commercial-industrial development within its boundaries may far exceed the burdens imposed on that municipality by virtue of the additional cost of servicing and policing the particular development which has located there. It is the theory of the Fiscal Disparities Act that the residents of highly developed commercial-industrial areas *do* enjoy direct benefits from the existence of adjacent municipalities which provide open spaces, lakes, parks, golf courses, zoos, fairgrounds, low-density housing areas, churches, schools, and hospitals . . .

Excerpts from Justice Kelly's dissenting opinion, with which Justices Peterson and Yetka concurred:

"Chapter 24, in any event, fails to pass the essential test of uniformity required by Minn. Const, art. 9, § 1, regardless of the status of the 7-county area as a taxing district . . . I concede that absolute uniformity of distribution is not required by our constitution nor by our case law. However, there should be some reasonable relationship between distribution of benefits and the taxes levied. In the present case, defendants' exhibit 1, attached to the majority opinion, shows many instances with little or no contributions by some communities which nonetheless receive substantial amounts of tax money raised in and paid for by other communities. While an argument may be made that these unequal distributions may change in the future, it isn't persuasive because in a number of instances the recipients of the benefits under c. 24 are so-called bedroom communities that have never wanted commercial-industrial property with its accompanying noise, smells, and unsightliness in spite of the tax benefits that might accrue to residents of those communities . . ."

Justice Yetka also filed a dissenting opinion of his own. Excerpts:

. . . It seems to me that if it was the legislative intent to encourage the development of industry in certain areas that do not have a high tax base and to help the areas which have large recreational areas, it would be proper to set up a metro tax district for the purpose of levying taxes to establish industrial parks in certain places and to aid in park and recreational area development and maintenance in others. But to levy taxes and distribute the proceeds so that a governmental unit can expend the same for general purposes seems to me not only a violation of our constitution but to actually inhibit sound fiscal management and long-range planning in those areas which have heretofore showed a lack of such planning . . .

## Burnsville appeals, without success, to U.S. Supreme Court

The closeness of the decision, with some justices not participating, raised some hopes of the opponents: "Patrick McInnis, Burnsville city manager, said today that he expects the city to request a rehearing from the Supreme Court, partly because of the split decision. If the request for rehearing is denied, he said, an appeal would be made to the U.S. Supreme Court."[148] The rehearing was requested and denied; an appeal was filed with the U.S. Supreme Court, and that appeal was dismissed.[149] Perhaps an indication of how strongly Burnsville wanted the law repealed is a comment by retiring Burnsville mayor Al Hall in an interview November 24, 1975:[150]

> He said one of his greatest satisfactions was the ruling by a Dakota County District Court judge that the state's fiscal-disparities law was unconstitutional, even though the decision was overturned by the Minnesota Supreme Court.

## Summary of the arguments pro and con in District Court and Supreme Court

Windhorst offered a concise summary of Burnsville's claim and the state's response in both Dakota County District Court and the Minnesota Supreme Court, in a July 1, 1975, paper.[151] Burnsville, he said, made two principal arguments: (1) that a metropolitan taxing district is not created and that local governments would be taxing property within their borders for distribution to other units "and that this procedure is unconstitutional because the benefits arising from the operation of the law allegedly are not distributed on a manner which is reasonably related to the burdens imposed", and (2) "the law violates the Minnesota uniformity clause because a tax is imposed throughout the metropolitan area to raise revenues for distribution to and expenditure by the individual governmental units within the area for local, rather than metropolitan, purposes."

He summarized the state's—and his—contention that (1) "the law did create a metropolitan taxing district and that the legislature could validly create such a district for the purpose of raising revenue for distribution to and expenditure by its constituent local government units" and (2) "even if a metropolitan taxing district had not been created, the law satisfied constitutional requirements because a reasonable relationship exists between the tax burdens imposed upon local governmental units and the benefits which accrued to them . . . The arguments in the Supreme Court were substantially the same as those which had been made in the district court."

## But the court test was not over yet

In 1975 a second court battle was initiated by taxpayers in the city of Shakopee and by the city itself. Shakopee is located west of Burnsville and according to the 1970 Census had a population of 7,716.[152] Shakopee challenged the constitutionality of tax-base sharing, now being able to cite actual taxes that were paid under tax-base sharing, not as in the Burnsville case where the challenge was brought before the law was implemented. The lawsuit was commenced in Scott County District Court.

## Tax Court rules against Shakopee challenge

Not until 1980 did the case come to trial. It was transferred from the District Court to the Minnesota Tax Court and heard before Judge Earl B. Gustafson. In his decision upholding the law, Judge Gustafson ruled that the Act in its application was not "hostile and oppressive" discrimination against the Shakopee taxpayers, which, he said, had been the only remaining question for the Court after the Burnsville decision. Judge Gustafson noted that, in ranking estimated 1975 taxes on a typical $25,000 homestead in municipalities over 2,500 population in the metro area, "Shakopee is 80th out of 88 communities, indicating that property taxes are near the lowest in the metropolitan area . . ."[153]

## Minnesota Supreme Court affirms tax-base sharing in Shakopee appeal

Shakopee appealed Judge Gustafson's decision to the Minnesota Supreme Court. By this time the court, which had voted 4-3 in the Burnsville case to uphold tax-base sharing, was much different in makeup from the court seven years earlier. Justice Otis was the only member of the 1974 majority still on the bench. Of the 1974 minority, two, Justices Peterson and Yetka, still were on the court, with Justice Scott, who had recused himself from the Burnsville case, presumably because he had been Hennepin County attorney when that case was tried in District Court, and Justice Todd, who had also recused himself from the Burnsville case. Chief Justice Sheran did not participate in the Burnsville case because he joined the court after that case was argued, and he did not participate in the

Shakopee case because he retired from the court before that case was decided. Others now on the court were Justices Rosalie Wahl and John Simonett, and Chief Justice Douglas Amdahl. The newest member of the Court was Justice Glenn Kelley, but he did not participate in the Shakopee case because he had not yet joined the Court when the case was argued.

An internal Citizens League staff memo reported on a pre-hearing conference May 20, 1981, before Justice Simonett:[154]

> During the pre-hearing conference, Rod Krass, Attorney for Shakopee, stated frankly to the Judge that Shakopee's objective is not just to have the law declared hostile and oppressive as it applies to Shakopee but that the Supreme Court's original decision in September, 1974, upholding the constitutionality of the law be overturned. Krass stated during the pre-hearing conference that the original decision was 4-3, two members of the Court not voting, and that many members of the Court, which made that decision no longer are sitting. Thus, Krass said, he's going to work hard to make this case a rehearing on the entire question of the constitutionality of the law.

According to the Citizens League memo, Justice Simonett did not challenge Krass' desire to place the entire future of the law in issue. A statement by Krass in the pre-hearing conference that Shakopee would be trying to get several municipalities to submit Amicus Curiae briefs to support Shakopee's case was a contributing factor in the Citizens League's decision to submit such a brief in support of the law, as it had in the Burnsville case.

Earl F. Colborn, Jr., Greer E. Lockhart, Allen I. Saeks, and David Graven prepared a Citizens League's Amicus Curiae brief to the Court. The Amicus summary:[155]

> The Act improves equally the quality of life for all citizens of the metropolitan area. It reduces the need for communities to engage in cut-throat competition for tax base, thereby avoiding higher public costs. It addresses the problem of distribution of tax resources without having to rely on state appropriations. Consequently, the Act is not affected by the

cutback in aids to local government. In fact, the need for the Act is greater now, as communities must rely more upon the property tax than they did when state aids were more plentiful. The Act carefully preserves to local units of government their taxing and spending powers. While the Legislature has produced a nationally-acclaimed piece of legislation, the Act itself is modest in its approach, with its impact felt gradually over time and not all at once.

Ultimately, the Minnesota Supreme Court did nothing but enter an order affirming the Tax Court decision, with no indication of how each Justice voted and with no opinions published.[156] Perhaps the Court believed that in light of the Otis opinion in the Burnsville case, nothing more need be said. Or perhaps they had no intention of tampering with a respected Justice's opinion. Or perhaps the Court wanted to avoid the risk of saying something that would encourage another party to litigate the case a third time.

## But the last judicial word on tax-base sharing had yet to be uttered.

As explained in greater detail on page 108, a separate tax-base sharing law, functionally the same as the metropolitan law, was enacted for Iron Range municipalities in 1996. The city of Cohasset, near Grand Rapids, challenged the constitutionality of the Iron Range law in Itasca County District Court in 1998.

## District Court declares Iron Range tax-base sharing unconstitutional

Judge Jon A. Maturi in Itasca County District Court declared the Iron Range tax-base sharing law unconstitutional on the basis that the municipalities on the Iron Range do not possess the economic integration and interdependence that is true of the municipalities in the Twin Cities metropolitan area and that the burden of the tax-base sharing law on taxpayers in some Iron Range municipalities outweighed the benefits.

## Minnesota Court of Appeals reverses District Court decision

The decision was appealed to the Court of Appeals of Minnesota, which on April 10, 2001, in a unanimous decision by Judges James C. Harten, Gary L. Crippen and Sam Hanson, opinion by Judge Hanson, reversed the District Court's decision and declared the law constitutional.[157]

The Appeals Court said the District Court should have taken into consideration the fact that the same communities covered by Iron Range tax-base sharing also share in taconite production taxes. "There is no question that taxpayers in the TTRA (Taconite Tax Relief Area) have benefited greatly from taconite production tax revenues . . . the Range Act, as an outgrowth of taconite production tax revenue sharing, satisfies the uniformity clause of the Minnesota Constitution," the Appeals Court said.

## Minnesota Supreme Court upholds Iron Range tax-base sharing

Cohasset then appealed to the Minnesota Supreme Court, which in a unanimous decision on May 2, 2002, opinion by Justice Joan Ericksen Lancaster, affirmed the Appeals Court.[158] Noting that taconite tax revenue sharing has "spurred more commercial-industrial growth in some communities than in others, it is reasonable for the legislature to direct that a portion of the increase in commercial-industrial tax base generated by that growth be shared among the communities within the TTRA," Justice Lancaster wrote.

As had been cited in previous decisions upholding tax-base sharing, Lancaster took note of the United States Supreme Court's reasons for judicial deference to the legislative branch on tax policy: "Since the members of a legislature necessarily enjoy a familiarity with local conditions which this Court cannot have, the presumption of constitutionality can be overcome only by the most explicit demonstration that a classification is a hostile and oppressive discrimination against particular persons and classes . . . [159]

# A flashback to a Colonial "Otis"

If "historic" significance were to be attached to the Burnsville deci-sion and the Otis opinion, it might be appropriate to note that another James Otis was given credit by John Adams some 200 years earlier for, in effect, starting the American Revolution. As explained in *Smithsonian* magazine:[160]

... the second president traced the nation's birth to February 24, 1761, when James Otis, Jr., rose in Boston's Massachusetts Town House to defend American liberty.

That day, as five red-robed judges—and a rapt, 25-year-old Adams—listened, Otis delivered a five-hour oration against the Writs of Assistance, sweeping warrants that allowed British customs officials to search any place, anytime, for evidence of smuggling.

"It appears to me the worst instrument of arbitrary power," argued Otis, "the most destructive of English liberty . . . that was ever found in an English law-book . . ."

"Otis was a flame of fire," Adams recalled years later. "American independence was then and there born . . . Then and there was the first . . . opposition to the arbitrary claims of Great Britain."

Todd Otis, son of the Supreme Court author of the opinion in the Burnsville case, in an interview May 13, 2020, said that, yes, his family can trace its roots to the Revolutionary Otis. The great-great-great-grandfather of Justice James C. Otis, Jr., was Ephriam Otis, a second cousin of the Revolutionary Otis, Todd Otis said. James C. Otis, Jr., himself was a fourth-generation Otis lawyer.[161]

# CHAPTER 6

## Protecting tax-base sharing: Resisting efforts to reduce its impact

### Early legislative effort to repeal

After tax-base sharing was found constitutional Dakota County legislators wasted no time in seeking repeal, with a bill introduced shortly after the 1975 Legislature convened. "The repeal will be sought by Sens. Howard Knutson, R-Burnsville, and J. Robert Stassen, R-South St. Paul, and Reps. Robert Jensen, DFL-Lakeville, and James Metzen, DFL, South St. Paul. Knutson was a coauthor of the 1971 law. Knutson said property taxes have become a less important source of government revenue because of levy limits and increased state aids."[162] The bill went nowhere.

### Someone else was after the growth in tax base, too

In 1969, as tax-base sharing was being debated in the Legislature, a different effort to capture growth in tax base was emerging: to help local governments finance redevelopment of properties. In that year the Legislature authorized tax-increment financing (TIF). It provided a way for local governments to pay expenses they incurred in preparing selected properties for new development, such as acquiring and tearing down old buildings, and installing new streets and utilities. Under TIF munici-palities would issue bonds to cover those expenses, utilizing increased property taxes or "increment" from the selected properties, once redevel-oped, to pay off the bonds. None of that increment would be available for county, school or municipal annual budgets until TIF bonds were retired.

Over the next few years the Legislature authorized TIF projects with different regulations in different situations: the Municipal Housing and Redevelopment Act, the Municipal Industrial Development Act, the Municipal Development Districts Act, the Minnesota Rural Development Finance Authority, the Port Authorities Act, and in several special laws governing local areas.[163]. Some TIF projects were required to contribute and some were exempt from tax-base sharing contributions.[164]

Shortly after tax-base sharing was found constitutional, the Citizens League began exploring ways to make TIF and tax-base sharing fully compatible. Leaders of the Citizens League knew that in absence of such compatibility the future of tax-base sharing would be jeopardized. City governments were far more interested in retaining a tool for redevelop-ment than sharing tax base. Optional approaches that keep TIF property within the tax-base sharing pool, while giving municipalities access to the growth in taxes for TIF purposes, were advanced by the Citizens League.[165] Legislation consistent with the Citizens League options was adopted by the Legislature in 1979, as described by the Minnesota Legislature's House Research:[166]

> . . . the municipality must include the value of any C/I property in the TIF district in determining its contribution to fiscal disparities. Under option (a) the TIF district is allowed to keep all of the property value and tax revenue resulting from growth in property value within the district. The municipality must contribute a higher percentage of its C/I value outside the TIF district to make up for the fact that the C/I value in the TIF district is not contributing. Under option (b), C/I property in the TIF district is contributed to fiscal disparities in the same percentage as C/I property outside the district, so the contributed portion is not available as tax increment to the district. Electing option (a) allows for greater tax increment revenues, but causes property taxes on other properties in the municipality to be higher than under option (b).

The 1979 action allowed TIF districts created before 1979 to be exempt from contribution to the pool until the districts expired, which in some cases was not until 2009.

In 1978, before the Legislature determined the relationship between TIF and tax-base sharing, the city of Minneapolis was attempting to keep its development districts from making a full contribution to tax-base sharing:[167]

> Experts disagree on the net impact of the tax-base sharing law on the development districts, but city officials are prepared to sue to see that a smaller portion of the tax growth from the districts goes to the seven-county pool.

> "This will have to be settled in the courts," said City Coordinator David Niklaus.

Today—with the exception of a special exemption until 2034 granted to Bloomington for the Mall of America—a city must include the value of any commercial-industrial property in a TIF district in determining its contribution to fiscal disparities.

TIF remains highly popular with municipalities, even though they can't use the tool to escape contributions to tax-base sharing. As of December 31, 2018, 408 units of government in Minnesota had 1,651 tax-increment districts that produced $230 million in TIF revenue during 2018, according to the Minnesota State Auditor.[168] It makes no difference whether municipalities are small, medium or large; rich or poor in tax base or income; central city, developed suburb or developing suburb; rural or urban. All types use TIF. Today, in fact, it's commonplace for developers to approach a city with plans that expect or assume that TIF will be used.

State auditor's data indicates that municipalities exhibit no reluctance to welcome and invest tax dollars in stimulating new development, which clearly indicates that tax-base sharing has not reduced municipalities' interest in attracting development within their borders.

## The promise and challenge of the Mall of America

In 1979, the same year that the Legislature made sure that tax-base sharing would not be diluted by TIF districts, the Legislature set in motion another development that ultimately would end up affecting tax-base sharing through 2034. In 1979 the Legislature approved the construction of what became the Metrodome sports arena in downtown Minneapolis, along with demolition of the old Metropolitan Stadium in Bloomington, across I-494 from Minneapolis-St. Paul International Airport, the current site of the Mall of America.[169]

It was immediately clear that the 99-acre old stadium site, with its prime airport-freeway location, was ideal for new development. The Bloomington City Council hired the Urban Land Institute at $40,000 to do a study of the site.[170] Foreshadowing the initial ambitious plans for the Mall of America four years later, the Institute recommended, as reported in the *Minneapolis Star*:[171]

> The institute panel said it is "essential that a 'unique' urban environment" be developed that allows pedestrians access to the entire complex "through major interior spaces and enclosed walkways."

> That complex could include12-story office buildings, 2,000 to 2,500 new hotel rooms, an international trade center, as well as high quality retail shops, restaurants and theaters.

How tax-base sharing would relate to major developments, such as the stadium site in Bloomington, were not far from the surface in the early 1980s. Minneapolis and St. Paul both were worried that major development at the stadium site could drain development that otherwise would go to the central city downtowns. But Bloomington said that because of the tax-base sharing law the central municipalities would benefit from stadium site development. The *Minneapolis Star Tribune* highlighted the controversy:[172]

> Planners from Minneapolis and St. Paul say initial plans for office space at the Met Stadium site indicate such growth will come at the expense of similar projects in the downtowns and that Bloomington has a responsibility to address the consequences of the development . . .

> Minneapolis and St. Paul officials say they don't want to stifle development but they do want Bloomington to consider alternatives. They suggest a scaled-down development or at least one with less office space . . .

Lindau (Bloomington mayor James Lindau) argued that Minneapolis and St. Paul should encourage developers to plan the biggest and most lucrative development they can on the Met Stadium property. He said the downtowns will benefit from increased money Bloomington will contribute to the fiscal disparities pool.

Possible use of tax-base sharing funds to help finance major developments was already being debated in 1984, still a year before the Mall of America was announced. A *Star & Tribune* editorial was critical of such proposals because of their impact:[173]

> The idea, which would have to be approved by the Legislature, is not unique—Minneapolis officials are weighing a similar scheme as one of several options for financing neighborhood development. But Minneapolis, so far at least, is only thinking about such a misappropriation of tax-base sharing money. Bloomington has gone further. It has made the idea a key part of its convention-center proposal. Not only would that pervert the purpose of tax-base sharing, it could have the effect of shifting the financial burden of a convention center mainly to those communities least able to afford the cost.

A stadium site proposal from Triple Five Corp., Edmonton, Alberta, which its owners called "The Eighth Wonder of the World", on July 2, 1985, captured the attention of Minnesotans as probably nothing else would:[174]

> A $1.2 billion plan by Canadian developers to turn the abandoned Metropolitan Stadium site into a combination amusement park, convention center and retail-office headquarters won unanimous approval from Bloomington city officials Tuesday . . .

> We will bring you the world's largest, most complete and most comprehensive tourist attraction and the largest shopping center," said Nader Ghermezian, co-owner of Triple Five . . .

The Ghermezian promise ultimately was realized. The Mall of America opened in 1992 and, according to its website, "each year, 40 million people from around the world visit the mall, generating nearly $2 billion each year in economic impact for the state."[175]

In 1985 Bloomington moved to seek outside financial help for the Mall of America:[176]

Yesterday, Lindau (James) and Belanger (William) said they justify going back to ask the Legislature for money because the development will have a significant economic impact on Minnesota tourism. They said they will ask to exempt the city from the fiscal disparities pool . . .

Bloomington's net contribution to the pool this year is about $3.5 million and that figure is expected to double next year, even if the site is not developed. If Bloomington were exempt from the pool, the municipalities that would stand to lose the most would be those that now receive the most money, such as St. Paul, Brooklyn Park, Coon Rapids, and Richfield.

Bloomington had been hoping to include a convention center in the MOA project, which was in competition with the city of Minneapolis, which was seeking a convention center downtown. In the month following the initial announcement Gov. Rudy Perpich was urging compromise, giving a new convention center to Minneapolis, and the megamall to Bloomington. Bloomington moderated its request and received some backing from the *Minneapolis Star and Tribune*:[177]

Lindau has modified his unacceptable proposal to help pay for the mega-mall project by exempting Bloomington from the fiscal-disparities law. He now wants the Legislature to exempt only the South Airport District, which includes the Met Stadium site where the mega-mall would be built . . .

. . . a bargain might be possible. The Legislature could decide that Bloomington need not contribute the full equivalent. The unique scale of this project may justify negotiation on the size of the city's contribution.

## Don't fiddle with tax-base sharing

Obviously, seeking taxpayer assistance would be highly controversial. Communities fearing damaging impact of new competition would be the very communities footing the bill.

"Which taxpayers should bear the burden of a property tax subsidy?" an internal Citizens League memo dated August 8, 1985, asked. " . . . the key question isn't really whether fiscal disparities or some other option is chosen. It is who bears the burden."[178]

In a fairly comprehensive update to its 1971 report on tax-base sharing, the Citizens League covered several issues in a statement to a House Tax Subcommittee on Fiscal Disparities on October 31, 1985. The statement emphasized that the law, as intended, was reducing—partially and gradually—differences in C/I valuation among metropolitan municipalities. The League reminded the House that the law requires no state aid, meaning that it imposes no burden on the state general fund, and, further, that tax-base sharing grows automatically every year, without any legislative appropriation.[179]

The League suggested several possible changes in the law:
- Phase out exemptions, including property at Minneapolis-St. Paul International Airport.
- Don't allow new exemptions, such as proposed for the Metropolitan Stadium site in Bloomington.
- Don't allow communities to escape making contributions by undervaluing property.
- Consider a variable contribution rate based on wealth of each city.
- Consider sharing of pre-1971 C/I valuation.

The League opposed both (a) sharing residential value, and (b) providing for a "floating" base year.

## Tax-base sharing was only a part of the subsidy question

Bloomington was willing to offer—and the Ghermezians were happy to accept—that the MOA would be covered by tax-increment financing

(TIF). That meant that property taxes from the development would not flow into the treasuries of Bloomington government, the Bloomington school district, nor Hennepin County until bonds financing public improvements at the property were paid off—probably 25 or 30 years. Bloomington wanted to exempt the MOA from tax-base sharing to lessen the overall burden of TIF.

The Ghermezians had ideas of their own about what subsidies they wanted, but couldn't garner enough support. As reported in the *Minneapolis Star and Tribune*:[180]

> The previous proposal—a package of special taxes and tax breaks to provide a direct subsidy averaging $15 million a year for 24 years, plus financing for highway rebuilding around the mall site—has come apart since the city and developer dropped plans last month for a convention center in the mall. The direct subsidy would be in addition to $140 million in tax-increment financing the city would provide.

> The city and Triple Five did not begin working on a new development agreement until about three weeks ago. And they appear at odds over the size and form of direct public subsidy.

The final package allowed a TIF for the MOA, kept the property in the tax-base sharing pool, allowed a piggyback property tax on top of the areawide rate that applied to the C/I pool as a loan (since fully repaid) from the pool for interest on highway bonds, but didn't allow a direct subsidy as Ghermezians had requested. State Rep. William Schreiber, Brooklyn Park, was credited in the *Star & Tribune* with designing the plan:[181]

> And Lindau's (Bloomington mayor James Lindau) proposal to tap the fiscal disparities pool for the money to build the highways could not survive the opposition of other suburbs, particularly the working-class northern suburbs that draw money from the pool . . .

> But so strong was the defense of the system that House Tax Committee Chairman William Schreiber, from the northern suburb of Brooklyn Park, sponsored a plan to use state money for some of the highway improvements rather than tamper with fiscal disparities.

Some tense moments occurred between Bloomington and the Ghermezians over the next several weeks. Late in the discussions when Lindau feared the project would die, it took a special trip to the Ghermezians' offices in Edmonton, Alberta, with Lindau interrupting a Florida vacation to participate, to get the project on line again. Big newspaper headlines proclaimed an agreement on May 7.[182]

## Municipalities seek to reduce amounts contributed to tax-base sharing

The Association of Metropolitan Municipalities (AMM) proposed changes in tax-base sharing to the 1988 Minnesota Legislature that might have appeared fairly mild at first glance. But what they proposed would have automatically widened the gap among municipalities in property taxes on commercial-industrial property.

What prompted the AMM involvement were some newer, fast-growing suburbs making contributions to the tax-base sharing pool who felt they were being unfairly treated relative to older suburbs and central cities who weren't required to share their pre-1971 commercial-industrial base. Meanwhile, more affluent communities continued to oppose the fact that they had to yield some of their growth to others.

The AMM's bill sought to address both concerns. It would have eliminated the pre-1971 grandfather provision over a 20-year period, so that ultimately all communities would contribute from all C/I property, before and after 1971. It also would drop the 40 percent to 30 percent, over a five-year period. At first glance it almost appears as if it's an innocent trade.

The Citizens League, original author Charles R. Weaver and editorial pages of the Star Tribune led the opposition.[183] It was quickly obvious that the bill called for a significant retrenchment of tax-base sharing. The drop in contribution from 40 percent to 30 percent was far greater than incorporating the 1971 base, which over time was gradually decreasing in significance. The bill died.

The Citizens League also highlighted a not-so-obvious fact that dropping the contribution rate *automatically* would result in C/I taxes going up in communities with higher-than-average C/I tax rates and going down in those with lower-than-average rates.[184] Thus the high-low gap between C/I property tax rates in metro area communities—which had been narrowing under the 40 percent contribution—would now widen. Such an impact, the League noted, would occur solely because of the change in contribution rate. It would have nothing to do with whether communities gained or lost tax base.

## Hennepin County: the big loser or the big winner?

No matter how one looks at the data, Hennepin County, most populous county in the state, is a big part of tax-base sharing. Since the program began Hennepin has been a net contributor. House Research reported that in 2018 Hennepin County contributed 52 percent of commercial-industrial tax base to the regional pool, and pulled out 36 percent. Anoka, Caver, Dakota, Ramsey, and Washington Counties all received more than they contributed. Scott County came out approximately equal in contributions and distributions.[185] The same general relationship was true for the year 2003 in an earlier House Research report.

If contributions to the tax-base sharing pool were regarded as insurance premiums, counties that consistently contribute more than they receive could be thought of as similar to homeowners who pay their home insurance premiums year after year without ever having to file a claim. They see themselves as ahead in the game, not begrudging their premium payments. Similarly, Hennepin County has paid its tax-base sharing insurance premiums faithfully (40 percent of net C/I growth) but to date has never needed to draw help from the pool because it always has experienced enough growth internally to lead the entire metro area.

That's not the way tax-base sharing has been perceived in Hennepin County, as the county board—and every other local government in Minnesota—wrestles with setting annual property tax levies. Hennepin County efforts to repeal or reduce impact of tax-base sharing were particularly intense during 1987-1991. Hennepin County commissioners approved a resolution in 1987 to "phase out the fiscal disparities base-sharing mirage and substitute instead a revenue-sharing formula that addresses the real causes of fiscal disparities," wrote Jeff Spartz, county commissioner, in a letter to the editor.[186] Among other comments in the Spartz letter:

No one has adequately explained why public purpose is being served, other than increasing the total pool, by sharing the inflationary growth in the value of, say, Southdale with the citizens of North Oaks . . . The $40 million in increased taxes paid by Hennepin County residents in 1988 could be better spent to help pay the increased costs of the real fiscal disparities—the ever increasing costs of the public safety, courts, mental health, welfare and corrections areas—rather than frittered away in subsidies to affluent communities outside of Hennepin County.

To help illustrate the depth of their concern, Hennepin County commissioners engaged in a bit of press conference theatrics. An article in a community newspaper includes a photograph with county commissioners surrounded by fake bank-deposit bags, which the article says represents fiscal disparities taxes destined for bordering counties.[187] An accompanying chart claims that Hennepin County lost $39.7 million in tax dollars in 1988, which was distributed among the other six metro counties.

Charles R. Weaver, having served in the Legislature and later as chair of the Metropolitan Council, and in 1988-89 a practicing lawyer, was a leader in opposing changes that would weaken tax-base sharing. In a letter to the editor, Weaver took note that "Hennepin County lists elimination or reform of the fiscal disparities law as its top legislative priority."[188] He went on to note that Hennepin County's valuation per capita with tax-base sharing is 50 percent above that of Anoka County, and that without the law the difference would be almost 150 percent. He also noted that 28 of 46 municipalities in Hennepin County were receiving more from the pool than they contributed.

In another letter to the editor, Jeff Spartz, by then chair of the Hennepin County Board, outlined several objections to tax-base sharing including (1) extensive use of tax-increment financing indicates that the tax-base sharing objective of reducing competition among municipalities for C/I tax base is not succeeding, (2) the law penalizes rapidly growing municipalities at the moment they need tax base the most, (3) the law subsidizes such wealthy communities as North Oaks , (4) the law provides an advantage to communities that under-assess property, (5) state school aid and municipal aids reduce disparities better than tax-base sharing.[189]

"Every other county in the metro area is like a hog at the trough, and they don't want their ration of swill cut back one iota," Spartz is quoted.[190]

A major news article in the *Star Tribune* on January 22, 1991, carried the Hennepin County concerns in detail, accompanied by a map of the seven-county metro area highlighting the tax-base sharing "winners" and "losers".[191] The article quotes Hennepin County officials who claimed the county would lose $61 million in tax revenues in 1991 to the rest of the metro area. The next day, January 23, the *Star Tribune* editorialized under the headline "It's beggar-thy-metro-neighbor time again".[192]

County commissioners Peter McLaughlin and John Keefe responded by outlining what they considered several shortcomings in tax-base shar-ing: (1) that inflationary growth, not only new construction, is shared, (2) the formula for distribution of tax base "is a crude instrument that fails to consider differences in the tax base needs of communities", (3) some wealthy communities prohibit C/I property within their borders but still receive shares from the metro pool, (4) some communities exempted in 1971 from making contributions still were exempt in 1991, (5) the program diverts tax dollars from developing municipalities at a time when revenue is most needed.[193]

"Please don't attempt to fix a program that is working well," wrote State Rep. Charlie Weaver, son of tax-base-sharing author Charles R. Weaver, in a letter to Gov. Arne Carlson, March 6, 1991. "The proposed 'solution' to this problem would send us back to the days when communi-ties fought each other over tax base at the expense of our environment. It would also hurt our children by further decreasing our communities' abil-ity to raise education dollars through referendum levies . . . In sum, any change to the fiscal disparities law would result in the rich getting richer and the poor being further harmed." Weaver's letter was also signed by 33 other state representatives.[194]

Aware of Hennepin County's opposition the *St. Paul Pioneer Press* editorialized March 12, 1991, "As others have observed, the Fiscal Dispar-ities Act is the glue that holds the seven-county metropolitan area together. It gives residents of every community a stake in what happens within the entire region, not just in their own community. This law should be preserved."[195]

More support came from Mary Anderson, chair of the Metropolitan Council:[196]

> I have always strongly supported fiscal disparities, even as mayor of Golden Valley, a "contributor" city. The law treats the whole region as a single economic entity, which it is. I regard fiscal disparities as an indispensable tool to help spread the region's tax benefits fairly.

> But fiscal disparities is once again under attack. The legislature is being asked to cap the size of the pool so it would gradually be reduced from 40 to 25 percent of municipalities' tax base growth since 1971. Also, other uses for that pool of funds are being proposed . . . Allowing a community to use a portion of the shared tax base for special purposes takes resources out of the hands of other communities.

Signed editorial comment from the younger Weaver appeared in the *Star & Tribune*, March 23, 1991, His words were more colorful than his father's:[197]

> The attitude expressed by Hennepin County Commissioners Peter McLaughlin and John Keefe in the March 9 Counterpoint article attacking the fiscal disparities law echoed the sentiments of Marie Antoinette who, when told that her people had no bread, responded, "Let them eat cake."

> Like Marie Antoinette, McLaughlin and Keefe seem intent on ensuring that the rich prosper while the poor suffer.

The Legislature in 1991 took no action to dilute or eliminate the program.

## Correcting the North Oaks problem

The Legislature in 1991 changed a feature of the law that was visibly irritating—but not as damaging as it appeared. It finally prohibited any community that didn't allow C/I property from sharing in the pool. North Oaks had been the favored whipping boy of tax-base-sharing opponents from the start. North Oaks is a very-high-income, formerly-gated suburb north of St. Paul that once had been a farm of James J. Hill, the railroad magnate. It was sharing in tax base, along with a few other lesser-known small wealthy communities. So the Legislature empowered the Minnesota Commissioner of Revenue and the Metropolitan Council to determine which communities should be excluded. According to a 2020 House Research report, the exact number can vary, with at any one time about six or eight communities removed from tax-base sharing.[198] But not North Oaks! It turns out that the city has some C/I property.

The so-called "North Oaks problem" was overrated. First, communities that finally were excluded had very low property tax levies. Second, their populations were very small and their homes were very expensive, meaning that their shares were comparatively small. Third, all were part of much larger school districts and counties, that were the chief beneficiaries of any C/I tax base that was shared with them.

Two exemptions placed in the law when passed in 1971 were more serious, and it took many more years before those exemptions finally expired. One exempted South St. Paul because of a federal redevelopment designation and the other exempted a redevelopment district that encompassed downtown St. Paul.

# CHAPTER 7

## Enlarging tax-base sharing: Efforts to broaden its impact

### Share residential tax base, too?

During 1993-1996 proposed changes in tax-base sharing were part of a larger package of proposed legislation affecting the Twin Cities metropolitan area.

Unlike the 1980s when headlines featured efforts to curtail tax-base sharing, headlines in the 1990s were more about whether to expand the law. Moreover, not just to expand but to introduce social objectives, mainly in the housing area.

State Rep. Myron Orfield, DFL-Minneapolis, was a leader in advocating that tax-base sharing be used to encourage more suburbs to accept low- and moderate-income housing. Orfield, first elected in 1990, was to serve five terms in the state House and another in the state Senate. A graduate of the University of Chicago law school, Orfield in 2020 was a member of the University of Minnesota law school faculty.

The breadth and depth of Orfield's initial housing proposals vastly exceeded modest legislation that ultimately passed in 1995. Orfield outlined the 1993-1996 legislative debate and action in his book *Metropolitics*. An excerpt from that book:

> Regional polarization and affordable housing are inextricably connected. The Twin Cities metropolitan region has a little more than half the affordable housing needed by the lowest income groups, and most of it is located in the municipalities and inner suburbs . . . Poor people who can find affordable housing live in it; many others must live in housing they cannot afford. In both cases, the presence of a disproportionate share of low-income earners and the housing they live in increases the demand for local services and limits the tax base of their communities, the main source of financing these services. [199]

Early in the 1993 session Orfield and Sen. Ted Mondale, DFL-St. Louis Park, introduced legislation that among other housing-related actions would reduce state aid for municipalities in the metro area that do not eliminate zoning restrictions and other barriers to low-priced housing.[200] The bill passed both houses but was vetoed by the governor.

In the 1994 session Orfield was chief House author of legislation that abolished the Metropolitan Transit Commission, the Regional Transit Board and the Metropolitan Waste Control Commission, and gave the Metropolitan Council direct operating authority for transit and waste control, which had that time involved a combined budget of $600 million and 4,000 employees.[201]

Also in 1994, Orfield sponsored legislation to enlarge the tax-base sharing pool beyond C/I by including some residential value, namely more expensive homes. By itself that step would have helped to further reduce differences in property tax burdens among metro area municipalities.[202]

Orfield's objective was much broader: he wanted to stimulate communities to invest more in lower-priced housing and to revitalize deteriorating central city and suburban neighborhoods. Via an intriguing concept on financing, he attempted to use taxes on the value of expensive homes in wealthier suburbs as a revenue source for (a) property tax relief, (b) financing lower-priced housing and (c) revitalizing neighborhoods. He would have accomplished such an objective by creating, in effect, a second tax-base sharing pool at the metro level that would have included the value of higher-priced homes. Instead of that value being returned to local property tax jurisdictions, the value would have been taxed at the same metropolitan rate as calculated for the shared C/I value.[203]

As the legislative debate proceeded, Orfield amended his proposal to let communities keep all *existing* value of homes exclusively in the local tax base, with only a portion of future *growth* to be shared (as was the enacted approach for C/I property in 1971). When faced with further opposition, Orfield removed the provision that would have kept the shared residential value at the metro level. In his final proposal, growth in value of expensive homes above a certain level ($200,000) would have been treated exactly as C/I, made a part of the metro pool and redistributed along with C/I back to the local jurisdictions. The proposal passed the 1995 Minnesota House and Senate but was vetoed by the governor.[204]

Orfield's plan to tie tax-base sharing to housing policy received support from Minnetonka Mayor Karen Anderson, who was quoted as suggesting that municipalities meeting a threshold on affordable housing would receive a larger share of the metro pool.[205]

Debate over Orfield's proposals had been intense among metro area communities. The North Metro Mayor's Association, representing 17 suburbs, "announced that they were tired of seeing most of the new highways being built in the southern suburbs, most of the poor from Minneapolis migrating their way and most of the new jobs going to their southern and western neighbors."[206] Northern communities cited data to illustrate that southern suburbs were paying their top administrators higher salaries, even though they had fewer staff and lower populations. Southern suburbs retorted that property taxes as a percent of income were relatively the same between southern and northern communities.

Two popular talk show hosts, future Gov. Jesse Ventura and future Congressman Jason Lewis, criticized Orfield in strong words, so strong that Ventura ended up apologizing on air.[207]

## Piggyback on tax-base sharing for Metropolitan Council's livable communities

Another bill with a modest connection to tax-base sharing was enacted and signed by the governor in 1995 and still remained in existence as of 2020. In the Minnesota House Research report of 2020, the legislation is known as the "Livable Communities Fund Surcharge".[208] In 1986, the Legislature had placed a piggy-back tax on the tax-base sharing pool as a loan to the city of Bloomington to cover interest on bonds for building highways serving the Mall of America. Because the piggy-back tax was on top of the areawide C/I tax levy that is part of tax-base sharing, metropolitan area communities did not lose tax base or revenue. The tax was applied exclusively to the shared C/I tax base on top of the C/I area-wide levy.

Since the piggy-back tax was expiring in 1995, the Legislature continued the piggy-back on top of the tax on the tax-base sharing pool but with a new purpose—to finance a tax-base revitalization account within the Metropolitan Council's metropolitan livable communities fund. Legislation specified the piggy-back levy at a maximum of $5 million a year, again without disturbing the normal contributions and distributions under the 1971 tax-base sharing law.

The tax-base revitalization account is distributed by the Metropolitan Council to metro area local governments "to investigate and clean up . . . contaminated land, ground water, or buildings . . . for redevelopment" As of 2018 the Council reported that it had granted more than $137 million to projects in 45 communities.[209] Largest grants in 2018: $880,000, to Minneapolis to clean up a 2.3-acre site with coal, petroleum and sheet metal contamination; $805,700, to Hopkins to clean up a 16.8-acre site with asbestos and petroleum contamination.

## Not as a cure for cancer, but more expectations for tax-base sharing emerged over the years

The Citizens League in 2004 highlighted the favorable impact of tax-base sharing on much of the seven-county metro area lying outside the built-up portions of the area, in what was classified as outside the Metropolitan Council's Metropolitan Urban Service Area (MUSA).

Bob DeBoer, a Citizens League staffer, reported "a new analysis by the Citizens League reveals that in 2004 more than $9.4 million in tax base will be distributed to communities that either have developed, or are developing, or could develop in ways that do not support regional planning because of the demand for a rural residential lifestyle."[210] DeBoer

said that policymakers "must take a closer look and decide if fiscal disparities should continue to support this kind of development."

Surprising headlines in the *Star Tribune* followed: "Fiscal sharing statute panned; Citizens League is abashed" was the headline on the first
page, with "What looked good in '70s has boomeranged since", on the
second.[211] "A new study by the Citizens League suggests that one of the
league's proudest creations is actually undermining regional planning
efforts to control urban sprawl . . . ," wrote David Peterson, *Star Tribune*
staff writer. "One way of making the program fulfill its original mission of
promoting regional planning efforts would be to redirect the aid to close-
in municipalities willing to locate hundreds of new households in high-
density settings along rapid transit lines that would reduce the pressure on
congested highways."

A source for highlighting tax-base sharing's "original" mission as
"promoting regional planning efforts" isn't mentioned, nor are the objectives in the law itself referenced. Objectives—absent any direct mention of
regional planning— were spelled out in the law when enacted in 1971 and
as originally expressed still are in the law today:[212]

(1) to provide a way for local governments to share in the
resources generated by the growth of the area, without
removing any resources which local governments already have;

(2) to increase the likelihood of orderly urban development
by reducing the impact of fiscal considerations on the location
of business and residential growth and of highways, transit
facilities and airports;

(3) to establish incentives for all parts of the area to work
for the growth of the area as a whole;

(4) to provide a way whereby the area's resources can be
made available within and through the existing system of local
governments and local decision making;

(5) to help communities in different stages of development
by making resources increasingly available to communities at
those early stages of development and redevelopment when
financial pressures on them are the greatest; and

(6) to encourage protection of the environment by reducing the impact of fiscal considerations so that floodplains can be protected and land for parks and open space can be preserved.

Of course, stating objectives in the legislation itself isn't really necessary. It's the specific actions called for that are vital. In fact, it's rare for other laws to express objectives, out of fear that judicial challenges could be based on whether stated objectives were realized.

Dee Long, a former state legislator and the first woman Speaker of the Minnesota House of Representatives, was serving as chair of the Citizens League Board of Directors in 2004. Excerpts from Long's letter to the editor, responding to the *Star Tribune's* article:[213]

> The research presented in the *Minnesota Journal* does not question or pan the law or the distribution of more than 96 percent of the fiscal disparities pool . . . We are not in any way reluctant to give the same scrutiny to 'one of the League's proudest creations' as we would to any other public policy.

While promoting regional planning efforts is not among originally stated objectives, the law has helped create an environment amenable to Metropolitan Council planning. Tax-base-sharing author Charles R. Weaver, who served as chair of the Metropolitan Council after leaving the Legislature, claimed that the Council's land planning act of 1976 never would have passed had tax-base sharing not been enacted.

Citizens League leaders in 1969-71 evaluated very carefully the implications of including every city, village and township in the seven-county metro area in tax-base sharing. They knew full well that all-agricultural townships didn't "need" a share of the tax-base pool. They also knew, however, that such townships in the metro area didn't have much population nor did they have large property tax levies. Thus their impact on tax-base sharing would be very small. Moreover, those townships were located in larger school districts and counties which would be the main beneficiaries, or contributors. Further, because there always was, and still is, a possibility that commercial-industrial enterprises would locate in an outlying township, it would be beneficial to keep such locations in tax-base sharing.

## Enlarge the tax-base sharing area?

Myron Orfield, who while a member of the Legislature, had tried unsuccessfully to tie tax-base sharing to larger objectives, particularly to stimulate low- and moderate-income housing, outlined another possibility in the book *Region: Planning the Future of the Twin Cities* that he co-authored with Thomas F. Luce, Jr.[214]

The authors called for more regional planning to protect sensitive natural resource areas in the seven counties within the jurisdiction of the Metropolitan Council (Anoka, Carver, Dakota, Hennepin, Ramsey, Scott and Washington) and four "collar counties" (Chisago, Isanti, Sherburne, and Wright), to the north and northwest. Orfield and Luce suggested that the Metropolitan Council, with its land use planning powers, be expanded to an 11-county area, including the collar counties. These counties, they said, "have become fully integrated into the region's housing and labor markets." To reduce opposition from the collar counties, Orfield and Luce suggested that the metropolitan tax-base sharing program be enlarged to include the four counties. They estimated that 77 of 88 cities and town-ships in those counties would be net gainers because of relatively low C/I tax base and total tax base per capita. No action has occurred on this proposal as of 2020.

"Most of the municipalities with the highest shares of sensitive natural areas are in the northern half of the region. Thus the part of the region with the lowest capacities to finance conservation efforts is also the part of the region with the largest amounts of unprotected sensitive natural areas."[215] Preservation of such natural areas is jeopardized because local governments think first of encouraging tax base within their borders to balance their budgets and aren't so likely to be motivated to preserve the natural areas from development, according to Orfield and Luce.

Their book is filled with multi-colored maps illustrating financial and demographic data for the 11-county area, including the location of sensitive natural areas.

## Discontinue property tax exemption for selected airport property?

The Minneapolis-St. Paul International Airport functions as its own city, separate from any surrounding city. Property at the International Airport never has been included in tax-base sharing. A similar exemption was granted to St. Paul Airport in 1996, according to House Research. [216]

"Some question the exclusions because their roughly $10.1 million in C/I net tax capacity would increase the pool by nearly $4 million," the House Research report said. "While airport property would seem to be an appropriate tax base for regional sharing, the unique circumstances make inclusion in fiscal disparities problematic. First, airport tax rates are not comparable to those of other jurisdictions because they pay no school district or municipal taxes. Second, under current law, the airports would receive no distribution from the pool because they have no population. If the airports were required to contribute to the pool, they would not get anything back, unless some alternative formula for determining a distribution were established." Without the airport property the total size of the tax-base sharing pool in 2020 is $477 million.

## Tax-base sharing comes to another part of Minnesota

The Minnesota Legislature in 1996 established a second tax-base sharing region in the state's Iron Range, encompassing part or all of 239 municipalities and townships in seven northeastern Minnesota counties. Duluth is excluded. The area coincides with the area that shares taconite production tax revenues. Mechanically the law works the same as in the seven-county metro area, except the base year is 1995, not 1971. The year 1998 was the first year of the law's implementation. A House Research report outlines why the Iron Range program was established.[217] The Minnesota Department Revenue prepared an analysis of the Iron Range program in 2014.[218]

Because of the sharing of taconite revenues within the area, proponents of Iron Range tax-base sharing argued that it was also appropriate to share C/I property tax revenues. Underlying the proponents' advocacy was the feeling that C/I development was flourishing in some portions of the region that had little or no taconite activity, and it was fundamentally unfair that these areas got to share in taconite revenues but did not have to share their C/I "wealth". Conversely, many of the areas most heavily impacted by taconite mining had become fairly stagnant in terms of C/I growth, causing them to look enviously upon their neighbors getting both taconite and C/I revenues.

The House report states that the program "has had the effect of transferring tax base from the commercially successful areas of the North Shore (Cook County and Lake County) and the western end of the Iron Range (Itasca County) to the older established cities at the eastern end of the Iron Range (St. Louis County), whose economies have struggled in recent years."[219]

The City of Cohasset led a group of Range municipalities that filed a lawsuit challenging the law. A district court found the law unconstitutional in September 2000; that ruling was overturned by the Minnesota Court of Appeals in April 2001.[220]

The possibility of an Iron Range tax-base sharing program surfaced at least eight years before its 1996 passage. A bill introduced in 1988 by Sen. Doug Johnson, chair of the Senate Tax Committee, was reported to be opposed by the Northern Minnesota Citizens League.[221] The League was based in Grand Rapids, which expected to be a net contributor of tax-base sharing.

At least one other part of Minnesota, St. Cloud, paid some attention to tax-base sharing, according to Orfield [222] Orfield reported that in 1996 a bill passed the Minnesota Legislature to study tax-base sharing in the St. Cloud metro area, but the bill was vetoed by Gov. Carlson.

# CHAPTER 8

## Evaluating tax-base sharing: Everyone wins, ultimately

### Initial analysis of results: as expected

The first analysis of impact of tax-base sharing was conducted by the Citizens League as soon as property tax data became available in 1975, with results published in the League's newsletter:[223]

> . . . the fiscal disparities act is functioning as intended: to reduce, partially and gradually, the impact of differential growth in commercial-industrial valuation around the metropolitan area.

The analysis found that municipalities that made the largest per capita contributions to the metropolitan pool of valuations (so-called losers) still had gained the most commercial-industrial property tax base per capita. The gain just wasn't as much as it would have been without the law. So-called winners still were at the bottom in per capita growth of commercial-industrial tax base, but not by as great a margin as would have existed without the law.

## After 49 years, all systems working smoothly

Analysis of tax-base sharing data for the year 2020, 49 years after passage of the law, demonstrates the same results as previous analyses: municipalities making the largest contributions remained highest in per capita C/I value, with and without sharing; the major recipients remained lowest in per capital C/I value, with and without sharing. The analysis was conducted by the author with raw data provided by Minnesota House Research.[224]

The law continues to bring municipalities in the metro area closer together in commercial-industrial tax base, partially and gradually.

Among municipalities with population of 9,000 and above, in 2020, after sharing, the city with the highest per capita C/I value, Bloomington, has six times the value ($900) as the lowest, Victoria ($156). Without sharing the ratio would be 13 to 1, Bloomington ($1,073), and Victoria ($84).

Municipalities highest in per capita C/I value, with sharing: Bloomington, $900; Rogers, $804; Golden Valley, $785; Roseville, $690; Arden Hills, $628; Fridley, $627; Shakopee, $616; Edina, $602; St. Louis Park, $577, and Minnetonka, $556. Nine of the above still would be the top 10 without sharing.

Municipalities lowest in per capita C/I value, with sharing: Victoria, $156; Mound, $194; Prior Lake, $214; Andover, $233; East Bethel, $242; Ham Lake, $261; Hugo, $265; Farmington, $267; Lino Lakes, $276, and Champlin, $288. Seven of the above still would be in the bottom 10 without sharing.

A total of 179 municipalities and townships contribute and share; the 67 municipalities over 9,000 population represent 90.5 percent of the total population of the seven-county area, 94.2 percent of amounts contributed to tax-base sharing, and 92.2 percent of amounts received back. Of the 67 municipalities, 25 are net contributors in 2020, with a combined population of 1,378,192; 42 are net recipients, with a combined population of 1,440,748.

The above amounts represent each municipality's tax capacity, which is generally two percent of market value in the case of C/I property.

Many municipalities with highest C/I per capita in 2020 after sharing were similarly ranked in the 1970s. For example, in 1976, the top 10:

Golden Valley, Maplewood, Eden Prairie, Edina, Shakopee, Blooming-ton, Roseville, Hopkins, Eagan, and Burnsville. The bottom 10 that year: Oakdale, Mounds View, Apple Valley, White Bear Lake, South St. Paul, North St. Paul, Crystal, Stillwater, Robbinsdale, and Shoreview.[225]

Minneapolis continues to be a net contributor, as it has been in recent years, and at $528 its C/I per capita is 14th highest among municipalities over 9,000 population. St. Paul, which always has been a net recipient, is at $422 C/I per capita, 27th from the top.

There's less to the impact of the law than meets the eye. As we've noted earlier, everyone contributes and everyone shares. Some munici-palities, at or close to the average, receive back about as much as they put in. All municipalities get some back. The total C/I value shared in 2020 is $477 million, which is not an insubstantial number. But every munici-pality and township receives back some of what it contributed. Only a fraction actually gets taken from the "losers" and ends up in the hands of the "winners". About 29 percent of the $477 million gets transferred to the winners; about 71 percent is returned to the municipalities and townships from which it was contributed.

Some concern has been present that townships, mainly in rural areas, shouldn't be included in tax-base sharing because being composed mainly of farms, they would be expected to be only recipients, not donors. However, as of 2020, 23 townships in the Twin Cities metropolitan area were net contributors to tax-base sharing, and 19 were net recipients. The urban-rural population mix of the seven-county metro area has not changed much since tax-base sharing was enacted. In 1970, 90.9 percent of the metro area population lived in communities of 50,000 or more; in 2010, 91.2 percent, according to the Metropolitan Council. In 1970, 2.5 percent lived in communities of 2,500 to 49,999; in 2010, 3.1 percent. In 1970, 6.5 percent lived in communities under 2,500 population; in 2010, 5.8 percent.[226]

## State House of Representatives non-partisan research keeping people informed

In the year 2020 it might be hard to find non-governmental organi-zations widely respected for their non-partisanship, let alone governmen-tal organizations. But plugging along in Minnesota government, ever since 1965 has been the Minnesota House Research Department, a non-partisan arm of the Minnesota House of Representatives, which is consistently turned to by legislators and others for the facts, period.[227]

Its stated mission deserves to be reproduced verbatim:

Minnesota House Research Department is nonpartisan: its services are available to all members of the House. The department strives to be politically neutral and impartial on issues.

Our Mission:

To help legislators and committees make informed legislative decisions, by providing information and analysis that is credible, accurate, and useful for legislative decisions.

To help legislators and committees develop legislation that carries out their legislative decisions, by providing expert and experienced help in developing and drafting legislation and in evaluating and understanding the effects of legislation.

To advise the House on legal matters arising from the conduct of House business. Attorneys in House Research serve as legal counsel to the House as a government agency.

Moreover, House Research's nonpartisanship has meant staff has low turnover, because staff doesn't get replaced automatically with changes in caucus leadership. Some respected individuals have spent almost their entire careers in House Research.

Such stability, non-partisanship, and knowledge gained and shared over several decades is invaluable for maintaining accurate information on complicated laws such as tax-base sharing for legislators, governors, others in and outside of state government, and repeated requests for information from other states. Thankfully, House Republican and DFL leaders have respected the role of House Research for more than five decades. Karen Baker, Joel Michael, and Steve Hinze, three recently-retired long-term researchers with House Research, are good examples. All joined the House Research staff in the 1970s. A recent replacement, Jared Swanson, is carrying on the tradition. Hinze in his retirement has helped Swanson prepare the most recent (2020) update on tax-base sharing.

Periodically—1987, 2005, and 2020—House Research staff has taken the initiative on its own to keep legislators and the public informed on tax-base sharing with detailed explanation, background, and current information. These reports are not sterile, dull recitations of legalese, but lively discussion. For example, the 2020 report mentions issues of public debate: "should the program continue to exist; should the areawide tax base be used to fund other programs; should other types of property be added to the areawide tax base; and should the program be extended beyond the seven-county area?"[228] The 2020 report should be the first place anyone interested in learning more about tax-base sharing should turn.

Further it discusses three obviously quite controversial "fine-tuning" questions": (1) whether property at Minneapolis-St. Paul International Airport and St. Paul Airport should continue to be exempt from tax-base sharing, (2) whether all C/I property, not only growth since 1971, should be subject to sharing, (3) whether factors such as crime rates, poverty rates, age of housing, and other "need" factors should be included in the formula for distribution of the areawide tax base.

The report also addresses rationale for tax-base sharing, mechanics of the program, historical and current data on "winners" and "losers" and a simulation of the property tax system in the absence of tax-base sharing.

## Lots of outside interest

Many interested persons from other states were aware of tax-base sharing from the moment the idea was first discussed. In1968, among non-Minnesotans on the distribution list for minutes of the Citizens League Fiscal Disparities Committee were John Shannon, assistant director, U.S. Advisory Commission on Intergovernmental Relations; Lynn Stiles, senior economist, Federal Reserve Bank of Chicago, and Harold Wise, chair of the legislative committee, American Institute of Planners.[229] Shannon's associate, David Walker, attended the Citizens League committee meeting December 12, 1968, when Warren Preeshl's idea for tax-base sharing was first presented.[230]

Charles R. Weaver, chief author of the tax-base sharing bill, gave a talk on his proposal to the National Tax Association on November 22, 1970.[231]

Possibly the most generous non-Minnesota send-off: "Unquestionably the Minnesota tax-base sharing legislation is the most innovative—yet realistic—attack to date on the fundamental fiscal problems of a metropolitan area,": *National Civic Review*.[232]

"Good Example from Minnesota", wrote the *Milwaukee Journal*: "Exciting, imaginative leadership toward resolving the central city vs. suburbs dichotomy in metropolitan areas . . ."[233] The *Minneapolis Tribune* gave its endorsement: "The metropolitan fiscal disparities bill approved last week by the Minnesota Legislature represents a major national innovation—an unprecedented step by a state to deal with urban fiscal problems."[234]

## Abundance of scholarly analysis

Non-Minnesota analysts of tax-base sharing were heavily focused on wanting to provide financial help to revenue-starved central city governments surrounded by wealthier suburbs. They might have not paid much attention to Minnesota's other actions on school aid and municipal aid, possibly having had little success with their state lawmakers in that regard. So perhaps the initial appearance of tax-base sharing appeared to offer more promise than it could deliver. Even in Minnesota the "winners" probably have gained less than they anticipated and the "losers", lost less than they feared.

Here are excerpts from a few scholarly studies:

"By reflecting the economic interactions and fiscal spillovers of local development and land use decisions in a market mechanism, it (tax-base sharing) ties the region together functionally without requiring political consolidation . . . In short, tax base-sharing offers an opportunity to make fiscal reform work *for* planning—we are not yet so well endowed with better tools that we can afford to overlook a promising addition to the kit.": *Journal of the American Institute of Planners*[235]

". . . the regionalization of sales or property taxes is not likely to reduce disparities among income classes very much, if at all, regardless of the inter-jurisdictional impact of these taxes . . . Thus, we conclude that in their most likely form, regional financing mechanisms will not be adequate to deal with the fiscal problems of large central cities and indeed may even exacerbate them.": *National Tax Journal*[236]

"Tax base-sharing appears to be an incremental step in dealing with both fiscal disparities and governmental fragmentation in our metropolitan areas, but it appears to be a positive beginning. Base-sharing must be viewed as a complementary approach, not 'the answer'.": *Public Finance Quarterly*[237]

". . . it is clear there has been a modest degree of reduction in fiscal disparities . . . However, more substantial disparity reduction will require revisions in the current formula used to distribute the areawide base. A revised formula should account for the uneven spatial distribution of population groups that tend to require higher costs for providing a given bundle of public services . . . A major commitment toward the reduction of horizontal inequities, however, also requires the redistribution of the residential tax base.": *Journal of the American Institute of Planners*[238]

"Base-sharing is by its very nature redistributive and it is so perceived. This is, perhaps, its tragic flaw; for all its potential in addressing disparities and rationalizing the land use planning process, unless and until local governments face some incentive—from within or without—to work together on regional problems, and for as long as political power resides with wealth, supporters of base-sharing face an uphill fight in state legislatures. Yet, as the Minnesota experience indicates, the interdependencies, and the potential for cooperation, exist." *Lincoln Institute of Land Policy*[239]

". . . anomalies could be avoided by the use of an improved formula which includes variables for median income and tax effort. Others have suggested a formula which includes a variable for the percentage of the population below the poverty level.": *Journal of the American Planning Association*[240]

"If central cities were able to share in the growth of the property tax base beyond their borders, their revenues would increase, but not very much. Its intuitive appeal notwithstanding, sharing property tax base growth is neither a panacea for central city fiscal problems nor an alternative for metropolitan governmental organization.": *Social Science Quarterly*[241]

". . . a long-run impact of tax base sharing may involve its symbolic value. Base sharing may create an awareness among metropolitan area citizens and local governments of the economic and environmental inter-relationships that exist within the area. The acceptance of tax base sharing may make future areawide cooperation easier and more successful.": *National Tax Journal*[242]

# CHAPTER 9

## Preserving tax-base sharing: Ongoing concerns and opportunities

### Last-minute effort fails in 2007 to give Mall of America tax-base-sharing subsidy

Although subsequently vetoed by Gov. Tim Pawlenty, the Mall of America almost received a tax-base-sharing subsidy from the 2007 Legislature, as reported by the *Star Tribune*:

> In an odd twist of events, the Mall of America's shoppers and business owners throughout the metro area could end up subsidizing the megamall's $1.7 billion expansion, courtesy of provisions slipped into the tax bill late Monday . . . the fiscal disparities tax would be increased to help fund the construction of an 8,000-space parking garage. [243]

The article cites Sam Grabarski, president of the Minneapolis Downtown Council, as saying that "he expects Minneapolis businesses to fight the proposals if the legislation is vetoed and then appears in another bill . . . I'm sure that when downtown retailers learn that some of their taxes will go to the Mall of America, one of their main competitors, then I'm sure they'll wonder if that was great tax policy. "

The *Star Tribune* in its report on Pawlenty's veto said the governor urged the Legislature to explore a different method of funding.[244]

The Minnesota chapter of NAIOP (Commercial Real Estate Development Association) was critical of the effort to use the fiscal disparities program to subsidize expansion at the Mall of America. Kaye Rakow, who in 2007 was director of public policy for the Minnesota chapter, in an email in August 2020 summarized NAIOP's position as follows:

> This proposal galvanized NAIOP's opposition because if permitted, would have increased property taxes on commercial-industrial properties, the pool's sole contributors, throughout the metro Twin Cities. NAIOP also objected to the proposal because of the absence of an economic analysis establishing a need for the subsidy and the satisfaction of a "but for" test. NAIOP Minnesota *opposed* any use of the fiscal disparities program as a funding mechanism for subsidizing local or regional projects, private or public. NAIOP Minnesota also *opposed* any and all diversions of resources from the fiscal disparities program which would have the effect of requiring business property taxpayers to subsidize the costs of competing private developments.

It might not have been the proposal to use tax-base sharing *per se* that produced the governor's and NAIOP's opposition. It was the method chosen: placing the entire burden on C/I property.

## The Mall came right back in 2008

Undeterred, the very next year the mall again proposed a subsidy from tax-base sharing.[245] "The mall wants an exemption from its contribution to the pool for 20 years, allowing it to use that money to help pay for the new parking ramp," the *Star Tribune* reported. Legislative authors were Rep. Michael Nelson, DFL- Brooklyn Park, and Sen. Tom Bakk, DFL-Cook.

"Nelson said any concerns he had about the use of the fiscal disparities pool is more than outweighed by the benefits of the mall's expansion."[246]

The Citizens League testified against the bill. "Last year's proposal would have raised taxes on all other commercial-industrial properties in the region . . . Just as bad, but in a different way, is the idea to exempt a development from the fiscal disparities pool. This would actually spread the effect beyond C/I property and on to homeowners and other types of property."[247]

The Legislature ended up giving Bloomington power to raise sales taxes at the Mall of America by up to 1 percent and taxes on food and beverages at the Mall by up to 3 percent, while leaving tax-base sharing untouched.[248] Sen. Dan Larson, DFL-Bloomington, said he would vote no because he contended the mall benefited the entire region and Bloomington should not have to bear the entire burden.

"Rep. Ann Lenczewski, DFL-Bloomington, chairwoman of the House Taxes Committee said (Gov.) Pawlenty favored placing more burden of the expansion on mall shops and shoppers and less on businesses elsewhere in the city," the *Star Tribune* said.[249]

In summary, efforts to use tax-base sharing to subsidize the Mall failed in 1985, 2007, and 2008. Was it three strikes and out? Not on your life!

## Big consultant study leading into 2013

A recurring argument of opponents to tax-base sharing was that some C/I tax base, particularly some retail, was requiring more city revenue to pay for city services to that retail property than the property itself yielded. So why, opponents argued, should such communities have to share growth in retail tax base? Taxes required by the city of Bloomington to provide city services to the Mall of America was a prime example.

Counter arguments were such that even if retail stores were not necessarily a bargain for city government, it was undeniable that retail, without children to educate, was a clear benefit for school districts. Municipalities continue to seek out retail development despite giving up the 40 percent share. Further, those communities able to attract significant C/I tax base usually seem to be better situated to encourage more C/I development than are municipalities with low tax base. Moreover, it always was necessary to remind contributors that well over one-half of the full amount in the tax-base pool was returned to them as part of their share.

To enlighten itself on the question of a suspected overburden of taxes from some C/I development, the Minnesota Legislature appropriated

$100,000 in 2011 for the Minnesota Department of Revenue to hire an outside consultant. The department hired TischlerBise, Bethesda, MD, that previously had done consulting work for the Metropolitan Council. The consultant was assigned to determine:

a. The extent to which the benefits of economic growth of the region are shared throughout the region, especially for growth that results from state or regional decisions.

b. The program's impact on the variability of tax rates across jurisdictions of the region;

c. The program's impact on the distribution of homestead property tax burdens cross jurisdictions of the region; and

d. The relationship between the impacts of the program and overburden on jurisdictions containing properties that provide regional benefits, specifically the costs that properties impose on their host jurisdictions in excess of their tax payments.

The final 223-page, multi-colored consultant report, with a host of maps and charts, probably offers more information in one place on tax-base sharing than one will find anywhere else.[250] It includes past and present information on metro area population, employment, income, and wages; the property tax impact on different types of property with and without tax-base sharing; how tax-base sharing works, and other information on laws relating to the Minnesota property tax.

The heart of the report addressed the extent different kinds of properties pay their own way in property taxes, both with and without tax-base sharing. The question of "paying their own way" involves comparing the cost of services provided to a given type of property to the property taxes paid by such property. TischlerBise went at it in a big way. Its analysis encompassed four major variables, with sub-variables in each:

—Type of property: (1) high-valued homes, (2) medium-valued homes, (3) low-valued homes; (4) condominiums, (5) apartments, (6) retail, (7) office, (8) industrial, and (9) tax-exempt institutional.

—Type of community: (1) central city, (2) developed suburb, (3) developing suburb, and (4) rural community.

—Type of governmental taxing jurisdiction: (1) city government, (2) county government, and (3) school district, individually by jurisdiction, and combined with overlapping jurisdictions.

—Type of sharing: (1) with tax-base sharing, and (2) without tax-base sharing.

The report includes charts that enable the reader to see at a glance the degree to which property taxes on different properties, in different communities, for different taxing jurisdictions are sufficient to assume the expenses of governmental services for those properties—with and without tax-base sharing.

Office and industrial property consistently show up as more than paying their own way, for all types of communities, for all jurisdictions, with and without tax-base sharing. Tax-exempt institutions, of course, never pay their own way, under any assumptions, because they don't pay property taxes. Retail is more of a mix, showing that it more than pays its own way for school district and county government, but not for city government. Most residential property doesn't pay its own way except for high-valued residential.

TischlerBise offers interpretation of the data at different points. For instance, here's part its comments on the data for developing communities:

The combined result is that there appears to be an 'overburden' under the current system when looking at individual nonresidential land use prototypes for this community, specifically with retail and office to a certain extent. This is true even though this community is a net recipient. Again, in this Developing community capital costs are relatively high, indicating a need for upfront infrastructure costs to provide for new growth. Industrial land uses cover their respective costs. When the program (tax-base sharing) is assumed to be eliminated, tax rates are assumed to increase in this community and more revenue is captured by the nonresidential development. Therefore, fiscal results improve and switch from an overall net deficit to net surplus for nonresidential land uses (except institutional). However, results vary by jurisdiction level where service impacts are experienced (i.e., city results for retail remain an overburden).[251]

With all the variables being brought to bear, the above comment illustrates that it was tough even for the study's authors to draw conclusions about the need to change or eliminate tax-base sharing.

TischlerBise outlined several "key areas of consideration", without making specific recommendations. Among the areas:

*"Allowing for exclusions of certain 'regional benefit' properties that generate high costs and serve as regional economic engines (e.g., the Mall of America)".* The report makes reference to 2007-2008 when the Legislature denied such an exclusion.[252] In a separate section titled "Overburden" the report states:

> For some levels of government, as evaluated in this study, certain land uses do not cover their costs when looking at them as discrete land uses. For example, retail development does not generate sufficient direct revenues to cover its direct costs at the city level both with and without the Fiscal Disparities Program. For other levels of government in some jurisdictions, the result for retail development is flipped. The overburden question depends not only on the level of government, but the locality itself. Levels of service, tolerance for tax increases, and the types of services provided are all contributing factors.[253]

*"Adjusting the 40 percent contribution . . .* For example, for retail in municipalities, the answer may be that 40 percent is too high. For office development in municipalities, however, the answer may vary based on type of city. And for other levels of government, there is another set of impacts. The answer to this question depends on many variables and is unlikely to have a 'one size fits all' solution."[254]

*"Including a spending need component to the formula, rather than purely tax-base driven."* The report notes that the state has separate programs providing direct non-property aid that is distributed based on need to local jurisdictions.

Release of the report appears to have been highly anticipated among media, legislators and local government officials. Shortly before its release, the *Star Tribune* ran a major article with a chart illustrating winners and losers. Excerpts:

Rising impatience in tax-rich Twin Cities suburbs over a regional program that takes millions from their budgets and awards it to less affluent communities will result this week in the most intense official scrutiny the plan has ever received.

A state report due out within days will examine whether the 40-year-old program known as 'fiscal disparities', which quietly shifts $500 million in tax base from one community to the next, is doing what it was designed to.[255]

In response to TischlerBise, Rep. Ann Lenczewski, DFL-Bloomington, and Rep. Jennifer Loon, R-Eden Prairie, said they intended to propose legislation to remove retail development from tax-base sharing.[256] Lenczewski said that the Mall of America in Bloomington and Southdale in Edina do not pay for themselves so the citizens of those communities must pay so nonresidents can come there to shop. "The report is technical and contains no recommendations that legislators could sink their teeth into," the *Star Tribune* said. "Loon said that disappointed her. 'This is kind of our first look at the program in 40 years and it would have been great to have some recommendations.'"

The report, however, with its 223 pages provided just enough weight in ounces and pounds, albeit not weight in specific recommendations, to give Bloomington and the Mall of America the momentum needed.

## Legislature exempts Mall of America from tax-base sharing through 2034

An exemption from tax-base sharing for the mall would finally be granted the fourth time around.

In opinion pieces in the *St. Paul Pioneer Press*[257] and the *Star Tribune*[258] Bob DeBoer, project director for the Citizens League, argued against the exemption. "To use the fiscal disparities pool in any way to fund programs or support economic development, public or private, is a misuse of the pool. To raise taxes on existing businesses to directly fund their competition goes beyond misuse to abuse", DeBoer wrote in the *Pioneer Press*. In the *Star Tribune*, he wrote: "If the fiscal-disparities pool is used to fund MOA, we will have started down the path of choosing regional winners and losers through the very mechanism that was designed to reduce competition and bring our region together."

Minutes before the Legislature ended at midnight, May 20, 2013, the Legislature with bi-partisan support granted a $250 million tax break to the Mall of America by exempting the Mall from contributing to the tax-base sharing pool until the end of 2034.[259] [260] The action provides about $9 million a year to pay for the mall's roads, water and sewer pipes, and parking.

An article in *Minnpost* placed the MOA action in context of several other business-related benefits granted by the 2013 Legislature:[261]

- $327 million for the Mayo Clinic, Rochester, MN, for its destination medical center
- Special tax-increment financing district for 3M to help build a $150 million research and development building at its Maplewood, MN headquarters
- A sales tax exemption worth $940,000 for Baxter International, Inc., to renovate a vacant manufacturing facility in Brooklyn Park.
- A sales tax exemption worth $815,000 for Emerson Electronics to help renovate a vacant building in Shakopee.

Details of the tax-base sharing exemption for the MOA were outlined in depth by Bloomington officials during a Civic Caucus interview on May 4, 2014.[262]

## Tax-base sharing: a sparkplug igniting discussion in many states

Rather than serving as a design or prototype for action in other states, Minnesota's tax-base sharing approach has served mainly as a sparkplug to help other states ignite discussions of possible fiscal disparities solutions. In years immediately following tax-base sharing being found constitutional, some states including Michigan, for instance, considered enacting legislation similar to Minnesota's. But as years went by the Minnesota example was cited to illustrate what an individual state can to do to address mal-distribution of tax resources.

There's never been a shortage of information about tax-base sharing. State after state has sent delegations to Minnesota. Countless news articles have appeared throughout the nation explaining tax-base sharing. More than 60 archived newspapers in Newspapers.com contain an identical Associated Press article about tax-base sharing in Minnesota by Jonathan Wolman in June-July 1977, including Fort Worth, TX.[263] Even as the 50th year of tax-base sharing approaches in 2021, states still are utilizing the Minnesota experience. Of the examples listed below, a study by the Government Finance Officers Association, an exploration by the Lincoln Institute of Land Policy, and a legislative proposal in Ohio were under active discussion in 2020.

**New Jersey Meadowlands**—A 14-city tax-base sharing arrangement for an 18,000-acre site across the river from New York City was enacted in 1972 as a location for a major league ball park and other developments.[264] For a history of the Meadowlands development: *New Jersey Meadowlands A History.*[265] Meadowlands as of mid-2020 remains the closest enacted example of tax-base sharing outside Minnesota.

**Detroit, MI**—In his State of the State address in 1976 Michigan Gov. William Milliken proposed tax-base sharing for Detroit and its suburbs.[266] The proposal died, possibly because differences in city-suburb tax-base wealth made it appear too much of a bailout of the central city. In 1985 a bill was introduced in the Michigan House of Representatives to allow local governments to enter into tax-sharing agreements but never made it out of committee.[267]

**Sacramento, CA**—In Sacramento, a proposal involved sharing the sales tax. "Regional tax sharing is becoming a controversial issue in California as the Assembly prepares this month to debate Assemblyman Darrell Steinberg's AB 680, which would share some of the sales tax growth in the Sacramento region . . . Imagine if the economic development directors of each of the 100 boxes in the region stopped fighting with each other, stopped sprawling against each other and actually found incentives to work together. Imagine how the local economy and quality of life might improve. Tax-base sharing can be a major first step in that direction."[268] [269]

"New legislation would require the six counties and 21 municipalities that make up the Sacramento metropolitan area to share some sales tax revenue, a key source of local government money . . ."[270] Steinberg's bill passed the Assembly but died in the Senate.

**Des Moines, IA**—In a signed newspaper article Richard S. Davis, executive director of the Polk-Des Moines Taxpayers Association, in late 1984 suggested tax-base sharing for Polk County and Des Moines, and including other counties.[271]

"It can reduce competition for new development by providing a means for communities to benefit from growth anywhere in the region," Davis wrote. "It assures additional valuation growth for municipalities lacking land for expansion. Since the majority of valuation remains with the city in which the development occurs, municipalities still have an incentive to promote commercial and industrial location within their borders. And, taxpayers in central municipalities can receive relief from a disproportionately high tax burden resulting from a declining population and valuation base."

The idea was endorsed by the Joint Economic Development Committee, made up of members of the Des Moines City Council, Polk County Board of Supervisors, suburban mayors and business people.[272] A bill was introduced in the Iowa Legislature, but no further action occurred.[273]

**Hartford, CT**—"The prosperity of the Twin Cities and their neighbors can best be summed up in four words: regional tax-base sharing . . . A tax base sharing program such as this would be an incredibly hard sell in Connecticut, just as other types of regional solutions are tough for turf-protective suburban residents to swallow . . . But increasingly, Connecticut will have to look to regional solutions if it wants to keep its foundering municipalities economically healthy, vital and relevant."[274]

**Pittsburgh, PA**—Three suburbs, Munhall, Homestead, and West Homestead, share 270 acres along the Monongahela River that formerly was U.S. Steel Homestead Works but has been redeveloped as the Waterfront shopping mall. The three communities have created a tax increment finance district for the area.[275] Ultimately, when the TIF bonds have been paid, the three suburbs are scheduled to share property tax revenue from the entire project.[276] [277]

Pittsburgh and other municipalities in Allegheny County share in one-fourth of a countywide 1 percent sales tax, with each city's share based on need.[278]

Pittsburgh area government and business leaders have looked closely at tax-base sharing but have concluded that concentrating on voluntary cooperation is the practical solution, according to David Miller, director, Center for Metropolitan Studies, University of Pittsburgh. In an interview on June 30, 2020, Miller noted that despite all the publicity and complimentary comments on the Minnesota version of tax-base sharing, no other state has enacted such legislation. Thus, he said, it is much better to concentrate on what can be accomplished.

In February 2004, to learn more about tax-base sharing in the Twin Cities metropolitan area, an all-day workshop was sponsored by Local Government Academy, Sustainable Pittsburgh, the Pennsylvania West chapter of the Government Finance Association and the Pittsburgh Chapter of the Pennsylvania Planning Association.[279] Some 80 Allegheny County business and county leaders made a three-day trip to the Minneapolis-St. Paul metropolitan area in May 2004 to learn more about the Metropolitan Council and tax-base sharing.[280]

In 2009 Miller was the founding leader of the Congress of Neighboring Communities, or CONNECT, "a nonpartisan initiative that convenes neighboring municipalities, including the city of Pittsburgh, that share borders, challenges, and opportunities in Allegheny County, PA. CONNECT is based at Miller's Center for Metropolitan Studies.[281]

The CONNECT agenda as of 2020 includes law enforcement-assisted diversion, economic and environmental development, infrastructure and utilities coordination, and public safety, health and human resources.

**Allentown, PA**—In 1999 the Lehigh Valley Partnership, a consortium of business officials, released a study by the Pennsylvania Economy League outlining the benefits of tax-base sharing.[282] "Among the expected benefits would be the stunting of urban sprawl, increased revenue for municipalities in need and the revitalization and consistent growth of the three largest municipalities: Allentown, Bethlehem and Eaton."

The *Morning Call* summarized a state Senate committee meeting in Allentown the following April: "Countywide asset sharing and school districts can help equalize the eroding tax base of inner municipalities, making them more desirable places to live and encouraging more people to stay or return from suburban flight, according to Allentown Mayor

William L. Heydt and other public officials, residents and representatives from private nonprofit agencies."[283]

Subsequently a new proposal was seriously considered--not sharing property-tax base, but--to provide for a 1 percent sales tax among Lehigh Valley counties and their municipalities, with the revenue to be shared among local governments using largely the same formula as in Minnesota's property-tax-base sharing. Ultimately the proposal was defeated in controversy over which units of local government would be included.

## National group highlights tax-base sharing in addressing fragmentation of local government

**Government Finance Officers Association (GFOA)**—The GFOA represents more than 20,000 members who are federal, state/ provincial, and local finance officials in United States and Canadian governments.[284] In a current (2020) report, the GFOA notes that some 90,000 units of local governments in the United States in 2017 spent cumulatively about $1.9 trillion. Tax-base sharing is treated extensively in the report, authored by Shayne Kavanagh, GFOA senior manager of research.[285]

"Given the vast sums of money and number of governments involved, it is reasonable to ask: is there too much *fragmentation* in local government and could public funds be better used if there was less fragmentation?", the GFOA report asks. The GFOA doesn't say so explicitly, but the timing of the report, given likely fiscal constraints on government as an outgrowth of the COVID-19 pandemic in 2020, seems most appropriate.

To improve coordination of resources between local governments the GFOA explores four models, (1) consolidation: combining units of government, (2) networked enterprises: creating informal relationships among public, private and non-profit entities, (3) government as a platform: finding the most effective service provider, whether public, private or non-profit, and (4) tax-base sharing: correcting for differences in local government financial resources.

The report explores how each model contributes to the goals of (a) spending less money in total, (b) reducing the per-unit cost of public services, and (c) achieving more results per dollar of investment.

**Consolidation** offers little in the way of achieving the goals and, in fact, local governments' tendency to keep an eye on each other's tax rates "holds total spending down and this force would be weakened by consolidation," the report finds.

A **networked enterprise**, according to the report, "connects previously separate actors in the pursuit of a shared objective and multiply their collective power . . ." Examples of networked enterprises are highlighted:

> San Bernardino County in California articulated a shared vision for the entire county and enlisted organizations from many sectors in this vision, including many local governments within the county.

> The San Antonio Community Vision is remarkable for many reasons, including surviving three changes in mayoral leadership, extensive community participation, and getting results on issues that the community cares about.

> Battle Creek, Michigan, created a community vision called "BCvision". It has brought together a number of public, private and non-profit entities and has been positively received by local residents.

**Government as a platform** finds "the most effective service provider, whether it is the local government itself, a private, non-profit, or another public organization, or if it is an activity performed directly by the citizens themselves," according to the GFOA report. As examples the report cites Englewood, CO, which merged its fire protection services with Denver, saving about one-third of its fire department budget, and Washington County, WI, which formed a joint public health department with its neighbor, Ozaukee County, saving the counties $300,000 in the first year.

The concept of government as a platform can trace some of its beginnings to Minnesota, in two 1970s Citizens League reports: "Why Not Buy Service", September 20, 1972,[286], and "Overcoming Obstacles to the Purchase of Service", January 14, 1974.[287] The introduction to the 1972 report:

We believe the expanding field of urban services would be better handled if more of them could be **bought -**by government. If, that is, there were a variety of organizations able and willing to supply programs, among which public bodies could choose . . . and if government were operating, directly or indirectly, as a strong and skillful **purchaser**.

**Tax-base sharing** is emphasized because it addresses what the GFOA report calls "one of the most important disadvantages of local government fragmentation", the differences in taxable fiscal resources among municipalities, school districts, and counties, usually encapsulated as "fiscal disparities". The report goes on to describe the Minnesota tax-base sharing law, "one of the most comprehensive and enduring solutions to fiscal disparities" . . . and that "There does not, however, appear to be any more recent attempts to create something similar."

Less comprehensive strategies, the GFOA suggests, would include (a) state revenue sharing, in which revenues are collected at the state level and distributed to localities "proportionally or progressively relative to taxpayers' income or wealth", and (b) changing incentives that local governments offer to encourage new development, but that "are not often effective in achieving their goals . . ." and "often simply cause firms to move within the region."

## Lincoln Institute of Land Policy considering a new study

The Lincoln Institute of Land Policy, Cambridge, MA, which had conducted a much earlier study of tax-base sharing[288] in the summer of 2020 was considering a study of whether communities that are net recipients of tax-base sharing are in better fiscal health because of the program and whether the contributors in tax-base sharing are fiscally worse off because of the program, according to Jenna DeAngelo, associate director. To undertake such a study, DeAngelo said in an email, the Lincoln Institute would need access to comparable financial documents for municipalities both before and after tax-base sharing was implemented.

# Ohio lawmakers considering voluntary tax-base sharing

**Cleveland, OH**—A bill for voluntary tax-base-sharing was introduced in the Ohio Legislature in May 2020 by state Rep. John M. Rogers, Democrat, and Stephen D. Hembley, Republican. The bill would allow municipalities in the greater Cleveland area to form Regional Economic Development Alliances.

"Regional Economic Development Alliances would be an additional tool through which municipalities could coordinate economic development activities, share services and collaborate to implement cost-efficiency measures," Rogers and Hembley said in opening written testimony to the House Economic and Workforce Development Committee. "What is distinct about the REDAs is the permissibility of alliance members to create a revenue gain-sharing program, through which pooled financial resources could be used to advance alliance purposes."[289]

The legislation is supported by the Northeast Ohio Mayors and City Managers Association through their "Regional Prosperity Initiative". William Currin, retired mayor of Hudson, a 22,000 population suburb, has been a prime mover for intercommunity cooperation for many years. Currin organized a visit for Cleveland area mayors to the Minneapolis-St. Paul metropolitan area in 2008 to learn about tax-base sharing.

In an interview in June 2020 Currin recalled a conversation during the 2008 Minnesota visit with the mayor of a city making a major contribution to tax-base sharing. Currin said the mayor told him that tax-base sharing has helped foster greater cooperation among Minneapolis-St. Paul communities because every city benefits from growth wherever it occurs.

Currin stressed that the alliances would be wholly voluntary, but he has expectations that municipalities will find ways to cooperate that will improve services while saving money. The alliance effort is occurring at a time when, because of fallout from COVID-19, state and local governments across the nation are facing major budgetary challenges. Currin, an economist, said that the expense of state and local government in Ohio represents about 13 percent of the state's gross domestic product but could be less if more attention were paid to inter-governmental cooperation.

A background paper "NE Ohio-Cleveland Metropatterns" that provides information on Minnesota's tax-base sharing and suggests its possible adoption in the Cleveland area, had been prepared in 2008 by Myron Orfield and Thomas Luce. " . . . the Twin Cities Fiscal Disparities Program is the best existing example of regional tax base sharing . . . In principle, tax-base sharing can be employed with any local tax. In Northeast Ohio, the primary candidates are the property tax and the income tax."[290]

For a week in late September 2019 readers of cleveland.com and the *Cleveland Plain Dealer* learned as much—or perhaps more—about tax-base sharing than most residents of the Minneapolis-St. Paul metro area know about the program that directly affects them.

Cleveland.com and the *Plain Dealer* had been offering their readers several installments on what was known as "Cleveland 2030, A Way Forward," to provide background information on ongoing discussions in the Cleveland metro area on creating a more inclusive environment for economic development.

As part of the educational effort Peter Krouse, an editorial writer for cleveland.com and the *Plain Dealer*, visited three Midwest metropolitan areas—St. Louis, Indianapolis, and the Twin Cities—to learn of innovative approaches those areas were trying to take, or had taken, to overcome challenges to making their areas more robust and inclusive. A half-century earlier the city of Indianapolis had merged with surrounding Marion County. In St. Louis the spotlight was on a current effort—unsuccessful— to merge the city of St. Louis with St. Louis County. In the Twin Cities area the subject was tax-base sharing.

Krouse spent several days in each metro area and returned to Cleveland to write several stories about each visit, including a week's worth about the Twin Cities area experiment. To read what he shared about the Twin Cities area, click these links:

- **What can Minnesota teach us about sharing?** [291]
- **Tax sharing in Minnesota means sharing tax base.** [292]
- **Twin Cities tax sharing creates winners and losers - or maybe everybody wins**. [293]

- **The Twin Cities success story began before tax sharing.**[294]
- **Liberals and conservatives embraced tax sharing in the Twin Cities**[295]

Krouse followed up with an article about response of persons in the Cleveland area.[296] In December he summarized findings from trips to Indianapolis, St. Louis, and Minneapolis-St. Paul[297]

The Krouse articles were intended to offer some of the background in advance of a 2 1/2-day conference, "Cleveland Rising Summit", in October 2019 that attracted some 600 participants. Several task forces on areas of community concern that were formed at that conference reported their results at a follow-up meeting in late May 2020.[298] Krouse highlighted 16 ideas for transforming Cleveland, although none addressed tax-base sharing.

# CHAPTER 10

## Working outside the "givens": The broader effect of the Citizens League

### Real change, not incrementalism

The 1968-69 Citizens League committee could have accepted the existing property tax system as is. If it had, the possibility of sharing property tax base among communities never would have emerged. But the committee had freedom to explore all possibilities. It had no obligation to honor historical precedent or traditional practice. The committee refused to accept the "givens" as traditionally accepted. Among the "givens" that were set aside: that a municipality where property is physically located has exclusive access to that property for tax purposes. Without other constraints, the committee had no hesitation about proposing an entirely new approach.

If the committee simply accepted traditional "rules of the game", so to speak, an idea that property tax resources in one metro area municipality could be available to other municipalities, without disturbing local government authority, would have been deemed impossible.

The citizen-based committee functioned independently, outside the "rules of the game" that would have prevailed had a group of professionals in the field were looking at fiscal implications of metropolitanism.

Any number of fields of human endeavor today are urgently seeking solutions to their problems—education, transportation, health care, public safety . . . the list goes on and on. Many factors hinder progress, including polarized lawmaking bodies. All those fields would benefit from new proposals that are not held to traditional boundaries that limit what solutions are acceptable.

## A respected study process

It's also unlikely that the Citizens League tax-base sharing proposal ever would have surfaced in the League's Fiscal Disparities Committee were it not for a carefully-considered and faithfully-followed process.

Key ingredients of the process:

- —Select topics for study from a comprehensive list of possibilities; avoid picking topics only because they are receiving extensive media coverage at the moment.

- —Concentrate on topics that are yet to be widely discussed in the community.

- —Express the nature of the study as specifically as possible.

- —Describe the topic in terms of the problem or opportunity to be evaluated, not in terms of some possible recommendation.

- —Insist that the individual or group undertaking a study first learn much about the topic, even those who because of their occupation or background might feel they already are well-informed. Avoid yielding to temptations that "we already know what the problem is. Let's get on with deciding what to do."

- —Conduct the study in as open a process as possible, keeping people in the larger community fully informed during the work. Such procedures will enhance credibility of the work and likely will stimulate outsiders to offer constructive suggestions.

- —Document the activity with detailed accounts of meetings.

- —Insist on giving honest appraisal to competing views, to help build broad credibility in the community and reduce the appearance that the outcome of the study somehow was predetermined.

- —Take special steps to assure that concerns of individuals and groups most affected by any recommendations in a study are thoroughly evaluated.

- —Concentrate on developing conclusions about the problem or opportunity being studied before moving on to recommendations. Conclusions are value judgments. Recommendations are specific suggestions for action.

- —Don't let conclusions take the place of recommendations. A study that offers a conclusion that such-and-such urgently needs to be changed is entirely incomplete without the development of specific recommendations for "how" the change should take place.

- —Before selecting a preferred recommendation, be open to several options. Warren Preeshl might never have offered his suggestion for tax-base sharing had he not been stimulated to share his idea because he wasn't comfortable with other proposals already on the table.

- —To build in some guarantee that the study will follow appropriate procedures, require that the individual or group preparing the study be accountable to a respected, permanent entity for final approval before official release.

The process became well-established during the time (1958-1967) that Verne C. Johnson, lawyer and former legislator, served as executive director. Johnson later moved on to serve as vice president and director of corporate planning for General Mills, Inc. Johnson was succeeded as executive director by Ted Kolderie, who during his tenure (1967-1980) affirmed the process, including stimulating national attention.

A national conference describing the process in Minnesota in 1976 was attended by 40 persons from 19 different parts of the nation. Growing out of that conference, a booklet outlining the process appeared in July 1976 in the National Civic Review, a publication of the National Municipal League, New York.[299]

## Selecting a topic for study

Early in the 1960s the Citizens League made a conscious choice to concentrate on developing proposals on its own, rather than simply responding to proposals advanced by state and local governments. It also made a point of selecting projects before they reached political party agendas, which also helped the League maintain its non-partisanship.

After selecting about a half-dozen topics for study each year—often picked from a list of 100 or more possibilities—the League developed written assignments, or charges, to voluntary citizen committees formed around each topic. The League wanted its committees not to assume any pre-determined answer, so the assignments were expressed in terms of the problem facing the community.

To illustrate a list of possible study topics, the Civic Caucus prepared such a list in June 2018.[300] In a November 2016 report, the Civic Caucus recommended improvements in the public policy study process. It included a recommendation that the Minnesota philanthropic community take on itself or facilitate the preparation of lists of possible public policy study topics to be available on an ongoing basis for individuals and groups across the state.[301]

## Learning before debating

The typical Citizens League committee always stressed *learning* before *debating*. Thus the first several meetings emphasized listening to, and inquiring of, knowledgeable persons on the subject at hand.

It was important that everyone on the committee felt fully a part of the assignment. Inevitably there'd be a mixture of (a) persons interested in the subject under study but wholly uninformed and (b) persons knowledgeable about the subject and maybe even occupationally involved. If too much discussion occurred early on, intelligent but otherwise uninformed individuals would inevitably be intimidated by more knowledgeable individuals, or simply believe they need to defer to the better-informed members. But when everyone sat through week-after-week of listening to and quizzing outside resource persons, it was amazing how quickly the uninformed were brought up to date. It was equally amazing to find that those who thought they knew all about the subject beforehand realized how much new material they learned.

Another advantage was that the committee came to appreciate early on that an important function of its final report would be sharing valuable background information—the findings—that form an essential basis for the conclusions and recommendations that follow.

Citizens League staff assigned to committees were deliberately not chosen for their professional expertise in the topic under study. They needed to learn as the committee learned. As they learned their background memos were much more likely to respect and reflect the current knowledge level of the committee members.

While reading materials were indispensable, it was critical, too, that committee members learn first-hand and be able to ask questions. Thus, most learning needed to occur via face-to-face meetings with knowledgeable individuals, known as resource persons.

## Keeping others informed of the committee's work

In the 1960s the Citizens League began keeping interested persons elsewhere in the metropolitan area and in and outside Minnesota informed of a committee's work, through what was called the committee's "Free List". This approach served several objectives. First, it provided Citizens League members who could not participate in a committee an opportunity to stay abreast of the committee's work. Second, it was a way to keep legislators and others informed, on the possibility that they might ultimately act on the committee's recommendations. Third, it was a way to keep other interest groups involved, who themselves might be studying the same topic. Fourth, it was a way to help educate, early, members of the media and others who ultimately might be relied upon to help explain whatever report emerged.

The "Free List" received minutes of committee meetings, which always were extremely detailed. It was not unusual for such minutes to run six pages or more, single spaced. Also various background materials were distributed.

The Fiscal Disparities Committee Free List included 165 individuals: 23 city government; 12 county government; 4 Metropolitan Council; 8

state government; 17 legislators (in addition to the legislators on the committee), 12 school, 11 media, and 82 others.[302]

Committee members plus the large free list received detailed minutes of the meetings with the resource people, so everyone could learn, including the absentees. In fact, Citizens League minutes were written primarily with the absentees in mind. Even though recycled paper was used, with text on both sides, the amount spent on paper, envelopes and postage was a significant investment for the Citizens League. By way of contrast, today it is possible to circulate such information via the internet without labor, paper, envelopes or postage expense, to almost a limitless audience.

The Fiscal Disparities Committee met 39 times between its first meeting, March 7, 1968, and its final meeting, March 13, 1969. The vast majority were three-hour evening meetings. Minutes of these meetings are included with Citizens League files at the Minnesota Historical Society and available for public viewing.

## Always remember: findings, conclusions and recommendations

The three most important words in preparing Citizens League reports: findings, conclusions and recommendations. Not that those precise words had to appear in every report, but the content had to include the substance of each of those words:

- Findings: What the facts reveal about the key issues under study. For example, how local governments utilized fiscal zoning to assure new homes would be valued high enough to "pay their own way" in property tax.

- Conclusions: The value judgments about the findings. For example, communities should not be utilizing fiscal zoning to deny lower-income individuals the opportunity to find homes in their price range.

- Recommendations: Specific proposals for *how* to address the problems identified in the conclusions. For example, change state law to permit sharing future growth in commercial-industrial value among all communities in the metro area.

## "If that is the answer, what is the question?"

Sometimes a Citizens League committee would become enamored with a new idea, irrespective of whether the committee had identified a problem to solve. Looking skeptically at such a recommendation, David Graven, one of the most active participants in the League, would ask: "If that is the answer, what is the question?"

All reports prepared by Citizens League committees had to receive approval from the Citizens League Board of Directors before the reports could be publicly issued. Again, sometimes to the chagrin of League staff as well as the committee members, reports would have to be rewritten. Staff spent the summer of 1970 re-doing a report that, after approval by the League board, became notable because it led to the "Minnesota Miracle" of 1971, with its comprehensive recommendations for changes in state aid to school districts and municipalities.[303]

Citizens League board members did not abuse their power simply because they didn't like a recommendation. If the findings and conclusions supported the recommendations, they did not challenge the report. Some members of the Citizens League board who supported the Minnesota Miracle report, for example, were aligned with a candidate for political office who attacked the report.

## The importance of citizen leadership

It was purely accidental that David Walker, assistant director, Advisory Commission on Intergovernmental Relations, Washington, D.C., happened to be in St. Paul on December 12, 1968, and sat in on the meeting where Warren Preeshl's tax-base sharing idea was unveiled. Two months later the *Minneapolis Tribune* reprinted a speech by Walker in which he noted the importance of citizen generalists leading in civic affairs:

> All our hopes for the success of the new federalism, therefore, depend on seeing the issue clearly, on getting the generalists to recognize their common interests, and on pushing ahead with the kind of governmental reorganization that will strengthen the hand of the generalists, as opposed to the power of the vertical autocracies.[304]

# CHAPTER 11

## Changing tax-base sharing?: The future of metropolitan public finance

### Are changes in the tax-base sharing law needed?

No. Major provisions of the tax-base sharing law today are almost the same as the law when enacted 49-plus years ago: exclude 40 percent of the growth in C/I property value since 1971 from each city and township in the seven-county metro area. Place that value in a metro pool of valuations and return the pooled amount to the municipalities and townships on a per capita basis modified for whether a community is above or below average in total value. The Iron Range law is largely the same, with growth figured from 1995.

A host of proposals to change have emerged: repealing the law, reducing the percentage shared to something below 40 percent, increasing the percentage, including residential property above a certain value, expanding the geographical area beyond the original counties covered, reducing the geographic area, exempting some property, ending the exemption for other property, including some measurement of household income in distributing the pool. Beyond denying coverage to select communities that prohibit C/I within their borders and exempting the Mall of America until 2034, the law is essentially unchanged and continuing to function as intended.

Tax-base sharing only partly removed rewards for fiscal zoning. Maybe more sharing would encourage communities to increase cooperation in encouraging economic growth. Or perhaps bigger shares of the pool could be distributed to lower-income communities. Aside from inevitable controversy such ideas would produce—and maybe even stimulate animosity, not further cooperation among communities—who knows what mischief might emerge in amendments that could be offered in the Legislature? Tax-base sharing never was designed to solve the all the financial ills of a metro area. It was designed to partly and gradually reduce differences in C/I property tax base among metro municipalities. It has succeeded.

## Are municipalities fully capitalizing on the implications of tax-base sharing?

No. Subtle improvements in coordination and cooperation, perhaps not even noticeable to the rest of us, might well have occurred among municipalities that participate in tax-base sharing. They understand full well that their tax bases are dependent about what happens in their neighboring communities, not just within their own city limits.

Nevertheless, the major expansion since 1971 in the use of subsidy tools such as tax-increment financing clearly demonstrate that municipalities are working as hard as ever on their own to attract development within their borders. Such efforts are undertaken by city councils for a variety of reasons, not just to gain tax base, such as bringing new employment to their municipalities.

Metro municipalities automatically gain tax base whenever and wherever new C/I occurs in the metro area. Shouldn't that fact stimulate inter-city coordination to promote economic development everywhere in the metro area rather than each city working only to attract development exclusively within its borders?

A non-governmental body, Greater MSP[305], specifically encourages economic growth throughout the Minneapolis-St. Paul metro area. Metro Cities, formerly known as the Association of Metropolitan Municipalities, represents the interests of municipalities in the metro area to the Metropolitan Council and the state Legislature.[306]

## Has an exemption for the Mall of America established any precedent for additional exemptions?

No. As noted earlier, the Mall of America (MOA) received an exemption from tax-base sharing from the Minnesota Legislature until from 2013 to 2034. What if more subsidy is sought for the MOA?[307] Or what if promoters for other mega developments in the Twin Cities metro area seek the same type of benefits granted to the MOA? Similar residential and non-residential developments elsewhere in the metro area should not have to subsidize competition at the MOA or at any other future mega development. Mega developments produce precisely the kind of land uses that individuals from other units of government in the metropolitan area will patronize.

## Should an existing piggy-back tax be expanded?

No. As noted earlier, a piggy-back tax on the shared tax base has quietly been in existence since 1985. Since 1995 the extra tax has been used to support a Tax Base Revitalization Account of the Livable Communities Act of the Metropolitan Council. The Council distributes the money on application from metro area units of government that need environmental cleanup of selected properties.

Only a portion of tax base in the metro area is subject to this tax, namely the portion of C/I property that is subject to sharing. Imposing the tax in that form likely had been very convenient for the Minnesota Legislature in 1995. The tax had been in existence for another purpose— a loan to Bloomington to pay the interest on borrowing for infrastructure for the Mall of America—and otherwise would have expired that year. The Legislature by retaining the tax avoided controversy that would have been likely if the tax had been new.

Aside from any political or procedural advantage some might see in the Legislature's approach, the real question is whether there's a logical reason to impose the extra tax on some properties and not others; and, furthermore, whether such an extra tax ought to be increased or ever employed for other purposes. Such possibilities can't help but be in the minds of legislators looking for a "quiet" revenue source. But, no, if the Legislature wants to impose a property tax for any purpose, it ought to follow straight-up procedures. Impose the tax in an open process where everyone can see what is going on.

## Should other states consider tax-base sharing?

Yes. Even today, a half-century on, there's nothing ancient or out-of-date in the metropolitan area problem of differences in tax resources among side-by-side municipalities. It's similar in all states. Clearly differences in state traditions and legal structures make it virtually certain that Minnesota's specific law won't be applied elsewhere.

Some aspects of the Minnesota approach deserve particular attention. When Minnesota's law was enacted, municipalities were required to share only future growth in tax base. No city had to give up what it already had. One needs to share future, not existing, tax base if the focus is on changes in incentives for future development.

Other factors, present everywhere, are differences in capacity to raise revenue. Some municipalities are wealthy; some, poor. Tax-base sharing isn't going to provide immediate financial relief to hard-pressed municipalities. Minnesota found that quicker results for adjusting revenue differences are realized through the state's formulas for distributing state-raised revenues to local school districts and municipalities. Despite the widespread term used to describe the law, tax-base sharing helps, but is certainly not decisive, in reducing fiscal disparities. As stated repeatedly, tax-base sharing affects the *capacity* of units of government to raise revenue. By itself it produces no revenue.

## Should a decades-old example of developing tax-base sharing inspire a better study process today?

Yes. It should. The tax-base sharing story illustrates the value of systematically following a well-established study process that can be every bit as useful today as in the 1960s and 1970s. There's nothing magical in that process. Just hard work.

It's not easy to develop consensus—let alone produce innovative proposals—on contentious issues of the present day. A bit of humility is essential. Participants need to set aside their own predispositions and spend time learning, or re-learning, the nature of the problem. It's so tempting—but so unhelpful—to jump ahead, saying, "We already know what the problem is, let's find a solution". Sadly, they don't already know that. Further, it's often painfully difficult to try to understand—not necessarily endorse—points of view alien to their own. But they need to try.

Then when time comes to make proposals, two steps stand out: first, insist that multiple proposals be on the table. Credibility of the selected proposal will be vastly enhanced. Second, it is so vital to avoid only expressing vague hopes for change. Proposals take on real life—and, further, believability—when they explicitly suggest the steps to make something happen.

Finally, a good dose of hope and optimism won't hurt. Is it really necessary to repeat the same old songs? "The country is so polarized that nothing can get done." "Those people are too entrenched in their views." "No one on this side trusts anyone on the other side." Give the process a try.

# CHAPTER 12

## Honoring the heroes of tax-base sharing

## Only heroes; no human villains in tax-base sharing

The story of tax-base sharing in Minnesota is really a story of people. Just heroes. No villains. The only villain, Ted Kolderie said, is the fiscal system within which local officials are required to act. " . . . municipalities . . . are forced into a kind of 'beggar-my-neighbor' competition with each other . . . each under a compulsion to try to get into its own borders the development that pays in taxes more than it costs in public services; and to force onto somebody else the development that costs in services more than it brings in revenues."[308]

Sure, tax-base sharing's history has involved opponents and advocates and those who were neutral, but all are heroes; none is a villain. The list below honors many of the heroes.

**John S. Adams,** retired professor of geography, University of Minnesota

**Alan Dale Albert**—author of definitive history of tax-base sharing 1969-1974.

**Wendell R. Anderson**—governor who signed tax-base sharing into law in 1971

**Charles Backstrom**—former political science professor, University of Minnesota, leader in early use of computers in tax-base sharing analysis

**Karen Baker**—former long-time House Research staffer, responsible for explaining tax-base sharing to the Legislature and the public

**Eileen Baumgartner**—former House Research leader who convinced Karen Baker to leave Anoka County and join the House staff

**Tom Berg**, lawyer, former legislator, supporter of tax-base sharing in 1971 Legislature

**Douglas Blanke**—lawyer for the state in Shakopee challenge to Minnesota Supreme Court

**Jerome Blatz**—chair, Senate Tax Committee, 1971

**Thomas Byrne**—mayor of St. Paul, 1966-1970, active in mayors' leadership group on taxes, 1969

**Donald Cleveland**—Minnesota House staff member during tax-base sharing debate

**Earl F. Colborn, Jr.**—chair, Citizens League Fiscal Disparities Committee, which recommended tax-base sharing

**Nicholas Coleman**—Senate co-author, minority leader in the Senate in 1971, later to be Senate majority leader

**Rollin H. Crawford**—mayor of West St. Paul 1968-71; active in mayors' tax study group

**David Dahl**—retired, Federal Reserve Bank of Minneapolis

**Jenna DeAngelo**—associate director, Lincoln Institute of Land Policy

**Robert DeBoer**—former Citizens League staffer and spokesperson for tax-base sharing for many years

**Debra Detrick**—planning analyst, Metropolitan Council

**William P. Donohue**— lawyer for the state in Shakopee challenge to Minnesota Supreme Court

**Steve Dornfeld**, retired, Metropolitan Council, public information; retired journalist

**Robert H. Ehlers**—author of minority report in Citizens League Fiscal Disparities Committee

**James C. Erickson**—member, Citizens League Fiscal Disparities Committee

**Curt Forslund**—lawyer for the state in Burnsville challenge to Minnesota Supreme Court

**William E. Frenzel**—House co-author in 1969; helped make tax-base sharing more palatable

**Gary L. Gandrud**—lawyer for Bloomington in constitutional-challenge to tax-base sharing

**Vance Grannis, Sr.**—lawyer for Burnsville in constitutional-challenge to tax-base sharing

**Vance Grannis, Jr.**—lawyer for Burnsville in constitutional challenge to tax-base sharing

**David Graven**—worked on Citizens League amicus curiae brief on tax-base sharing to Minnesota Supreme Court

**Robert D. Heacock, Jr.**—lawyer for Bloomington in constitutional challenge to tax-base sharing

**Julie Herlands**—chief author, TischlerBise report on tax-base sharing

**Pahoua Yang Hoffman**—Citizens League executive director, 2017-2020

**Curt Johnson**—Citizens League executive director, 1980-1991

**Verne C. Johnson**—Citizens League executive director, 1958-1967

**John Earl Haynes**—staff tax advisor to Gov. Wendell R. Anderson in 1971

**Shayne Kavanagh**—senior manager of research, Government Finance Officers Association

**Sean Kershaw**—Citizens League executive director, 2003-2017

**Gene Knaff**—long-time economist, Metropolitan Council, now retired

**Howard Knutson**—co-author on tax-base sharing bill in 1971

**Ted Kolderie**—Citizens League executive director, 1967-1980

**Rod Krass**—represented Shakopee and Cohasset in challenges to tax-base sharing

**Charles R. Lefebvre**—Anoka County auditor 1970-1990, administrative auditor for tax-base sharing

**Ann Lenczewski**—former chair of House Tax Committee; helped craft tax-exemption for Mall of America

**Ernie Lindstrom**—Republican House Majority Leader in 1971 Minnesota Legislature

**Greer E. Lockhart**— worked on Citizens League amicus curiae briefs on tax-base sharing to Minnesota Supreme Court

**Thomas Luce**—author of tax-base sharing studies, Institute for Metropolitan Opportunity, Law School, University of Minnesota

**David Miller**, founder, Congress of Neighboring Communities, Pittsburgh, PA

**Allen Muglia**—headed Metropolitan Council fiscal studies in 1971

**Arthur Naftalin**—mayor of Minneapolis, 1961-1969, active in mayors' tax study group on taxes

**Myron Orfield**—advocate for expansion of tax-base sharing, as legislator, author, and law professor

**James C. Otis, Jr.**—Justice of the Minnesota Supreme Court who wrote the decision upholding constitutionality of tax-base sharing

**Todd Otis**—son of James C. Otis, Jr., provided information Otis family history

**Gloria Pinke**—worked on tax-base sharing data for Dakota County assessor for 45 years

**Wayne G. Popham**—chief author in the Senate of tax-base sharing legislation, 1969-71

**F. Warren Preeshl**—originated the idea of tax-base sharing in Citizens League Fiscal Disparities Committee

**Kaye Eleanor Rakow**—Public Policy Director, NAIOP, the commercial real estate development association, who fought the effort to use the fiscal disparities program to subsidize expansion at the Mall of America.

**Andrew Reschovsky**—consultant to Metropolitan Council on tax-base sharing in 1970s.

**Ann Rest**—State Senator, tax authority, in Legislature during most of tax-base sharing's history

**Martin Sabo**—House co-author of tax-base sharing bill, minority leader in the House in 1971, later to be House Speaker

**Dana Schroeder**, former editor, *Minnesota Journal,* author of several tax-base-sharing updates

**Allen I. Saeks**—lawyer for Citizens League on amicus curiae briefs in Burnsville and Shakopee court challenges

**Jerry Silkey**— former director of research, Minnesota Department of Revenue

**Jared Swanson**—House Research staffer, author of tax-base sharing report in 2020

**Judy Vrdolak**—longtime employee in Anoka County Auditor's office

**Charles R. Weaver**—chief advocate for tax-base sharing and chief author in the House 1969-71

**Charles R. (Charlie) Weaver, Jr.**—former legislator, defender of tax-base sharing, son of Charles R. Weaver

**Tom Weaver**, former administrator, Metropolitan Council, son of Charles R. Weaver

**John W. Windhorst, Jr.**—drafted original bill for tax-base sharing; represented Metropolitan Council in court cases

**Arthur B. Whitney**—supported minority report on tax-base sharing in Citizens League Fiscal Disparities Committee, but wrote supportive memo on its workability

**Lyle Wray,** Citizens League executive director, 1992-2003

Not to be otherwise forgotten are Citizens League clerical and professional staff who served at various times in the late 1960s and 1970s: Judy Alnes, Steve Alnes, Paula Ballanger, George Bauman, May Marie Benson, Bill Blazar, Jean Bosch, Jim Carney, Neill T. Carter, Cal Clark, Donna Daniels, Jody Hauer, Philip Jenni, Ted Kolderie, Dawn Latulippe, Joann

Latulippe, Andy Lindberg, Hertha Lutz, Mary Maranowski, Marina Munoz Lyon, Laura Merriam, Eric Premark, Berry Richards, Brad Richards, Richard Sadler, Dana Schroeder, Jon Schroeder, Theresa Schmieg, Clarence Shallbetter, Bonnie Sipkins, Glen Skovholt, Irma Sletten, Vera Sparkes, Margo Stark, Allan Tingley, Peter Vanderpoel, Bob de la Vega, and Deborah Zweber.

## Recent audio recordings with some tax-base sharing leaders are available

During 2019 and 2020 informal conference calls with tax-base sharing leaders past and present were conducted and recorded online. The recordings, averaging about one hour each:

- April 5, 2020, Karen Baker, Steve Hinze, Jared Swanson and others: https://fccdl.in/i4O3Oeg00c
- February 17, 2020, Gene Knaff, Andrew Reschovsky: https://fccdl.in/IA9src551A
- January 20, 2020, John Earl Haynes: https://fccdl.in/idAWXlYhMI
- January 13, 2020, Alan Dale Albert: https://fccdl.in/3blIR0UNQw
- January 10, 2020, Rollin H. Crawford: https://fccdl.in/H9HCFhCXPo
- January 6, 2020, Gilje, Kolderie, Hinze, Windhorst, Schroeder: https://fccdl.in/ETWJghWsaQ
- December 17, 2019, Charlie and Tom Weaver: https://fccdl.in/p2DXlCXYiy
- December 16, 2019, Peter Krouse: https://fccdl.in/Bub4twMVi0
- December 13, 2019, Andrew Reschovsky: https://fccdl.in/Y9MLk4RbZU.
- November 22, 2019, Myron Orfield: https://fccdl.in/KOhUngGsBY
- November 19, 2019, Ted Kolderie: https://fccdl.in/WdREytzKk9

- November 15, 2019, Steve Hinze and Karen Baker: https://fccdl.in/BgvlcMj5Xz
- November 4, 2019, Wayne Popham: https://fccdl.in/rLJ1sJTT4w
- October 31, 2019, Jack Windhorst: https://fccdl.in/mFpNFQPEgU
- October 19, 2019, Steve Dornfeld: https://fccdl.in/QwHtMUtBkr

# Appendix

## Map of Minneapolis-St. Paul metropolitan tax-base sharing area

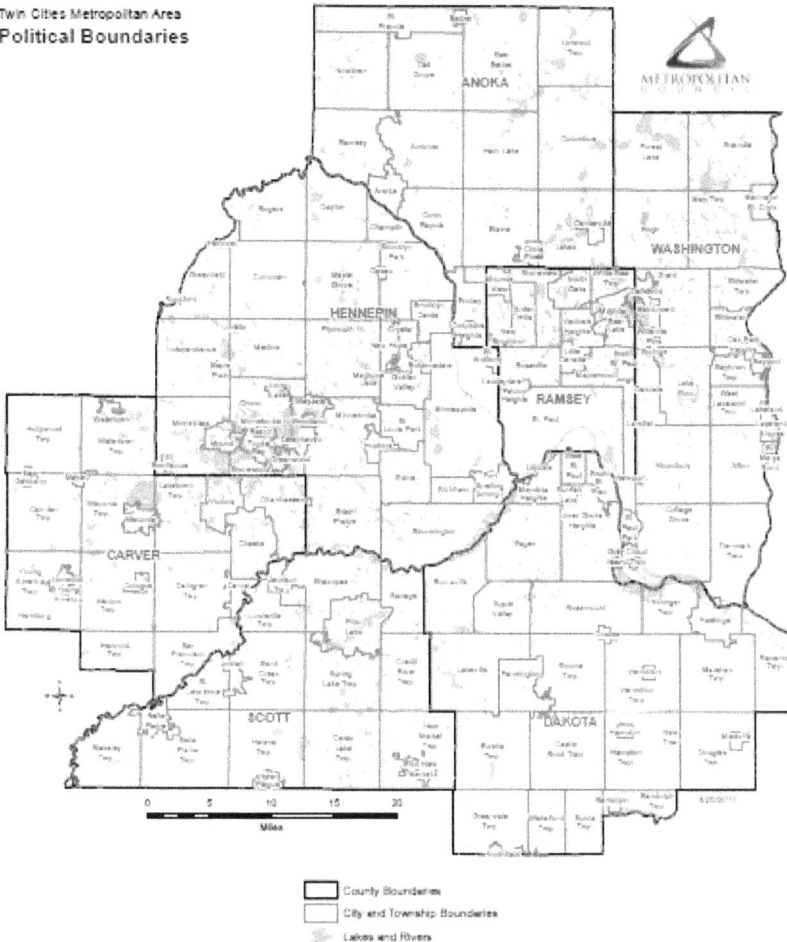

Twin Cities Metropolitan Area
Political Boundaries

# Map of Iron Range tax-base sharing area

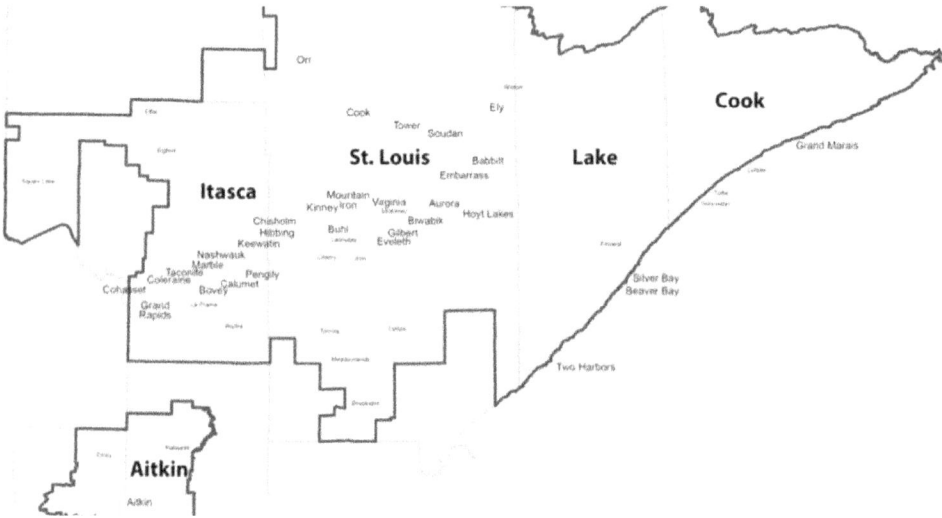

## Speakers at Citizens League Fiscal Disparities Committee 1968-69[309]

**Outside experts:** Lynn A. Stiles, senior economist, Federal Reserve Bank of Chicago; Wilbur Thompson, professor of economics, Wayne State University, Detroit, MI.

**City government:** John Pidgeon, Bloomington city manager; R. W. Turnlund, Roseville villlage manager; Rollin H. Crawford, mayor, West St. Paul; Joseph P. Summers, corporation counsel, St. Paul; Dan Cohen, president, Minneapolis City Council;

**County government:** William Koniarski, chair, Scott County Board; Bernard F. Schneider, Carver County Board member

**Legislators:** State Rep. Howard Albertson, Stillwater; State Rep. Ernest Lindstrom, Richfield; State Rep. Robert W. Johnson, St. Paul; former state Rep. D. D. Wozniak, St. Paul.

**State government:** Rolland F. Hatfield, state commissioner of administration; Arthur Roemer, deputy state commissioner of taxation; Duane Mattheis, state commissioner of education; S. Walter Harvey, research director, state department of education.

**Schools:** John B. Davis, Jr., superintendent, Minneapolis; Gordon E. Miniclier, assistant superintendent, St. Paul; Marshall Hankerson, superintendent, Centennial; Russell Anderson, superintendent, West St. Paul; George J. Greenawalt, superintendent, Hopkins; Lloyd C. Nielsen, superintendent, Roseville; Spencer Myers, superintendent, Edina; Donald Prior, business manager, Edina; Fred Atkinson, superintendent, Bloomington; Ernest M. Thomsen, superintendent, White Bear Lake; Erling O. Johnson, superintendent, Anoka.

**Private sector:** Larry Laukka, vice-president and marketing manager, Pemtom, Inc.; Howard Dahlgren, Midwest Planning and Research, Inc.; D. W. Angland, vice president and manager of planning, Northern States Power Co.

The humble, patient, understanding, cooperative assistance from countless other individuals in Minnesota's public and private sector was essential to the work of the Citizens League Fiscal Disparities Committee and its staff. The ultimate reasons for and legitimacy of tax-base sharing would not have emerged otherwise. Citizens League staff members knew how to ask questions and how to communicate their learning orally and in writing to others, but they most definitely were not experts in their own right. In fact, Citizens League leaders hired generalists to work with volunteers. Both would learn together. The staff didn't teach the volunteers.

Thus scores of now-forgotten Minnesotans have made invaluable contributions to the Citizens League. Heads of organizations and departments were part of this group, as well as untold assistants in this or that office in school districts, municipalities, counties, state government, colleges and universities, and non-profit and for-profit organizations. These people received draft memos, phone calls and requests from Citizens League staff for interviews to explain—often again and again—how something worked or what its implications were.

# A flurry of Citizens League activity

The metropolitan tax-base sharing report emerged during a time of intensive Citizens League activity on a host of topics. The tax-base sharing report was only one of some 40 major Citizens League reports issued between 1963—when the Citizens League began utilizing ad hoc committees with major reports for each subject under study, rather than standing committees as in the past—and mid-1971, when tax-base sharing was enacted into law. Many more additional Citizens League statements were also issued. All may be accessed at the Citizens League website.[310]

## Courts and Public Safety

- Hennepin County Courts Reorganization, February 13, 1963, James L. Hetland, Jr., and Philip Neville, co-chairs
- Should the Minneapolis Workhouse be Transferred to Hennepin County?, March 17, 1965, John W. Pulver, chair
- Minneapolis-Hennepin County Jails, July 13, 1966, C. Paul Jones, chair
- Getting Answers for the Control of Crime, December 22, 1970, Paul H. Hauge, chair

## Government Structure

- The Minnesota Municipal Commission: Where Now?, March 17, 1965, Greer Lockhart, chair
- Local Consent Requirements to State Law, April 1965, Wallace Neal, Jr., chair
- The Future Role of the Metropolitan Planning Commission, May 10, 1965, Archibald Spencer, chair
- Hennepin County Government Reorganization, December 2, 1966, James L. Hetland, Jr., chair
- A Metropolitan Council for the Twin Cities Area, March 2, 1967, Charles H. Clay, chair
- Organization for State Policy-making: 29 Proposals for Strengthening the Minnesota Legislature, March 2, 1968, Peter H. Seed, chair
- Metropolitan Policy and Metropolitan Development, October 14, 1968, John Finnegan and Greer Lockhart, co-chairs

- Who Will Help Us Get Action? A Proposal to Answer the Appeal for Political Leadership in Solving the Problems Confronting the City of Minneapolis , April 1969)
- Suburbs in the City: Ways to Expand Participation and Representation in Minneapolis Government, May 13, 1970, James L. Weaver, chair

## Education

- Minneapolis School System Building Needs, October 29, 1963, James H. Hetland, Jr., chair
- Community Colleges for the Twin Cities area, June 28, 1967, John W. Windhorst, chair
- Stretching the School Salary Dollar, July 30, 1969, John W. Mooty, chair
- Resolving Teacher-School Board Disputes, March 24, 1971, Roger L. Hale, chair
- An 'Urban College': New Kinds of Students on a New Kind of 'Campus', April 15, 1971, Allen I. Saeks, chair

## Elections

- Needed Improvements in Voting Procedures, March 2, 1966, James L. Weaver, chair

## Environment

- Twin Cities Metropolitan Area Sewage Needs, April 29, 1965, Charles H. Clay, chair
- Metropolitan Mosquito Control District, May 4 1966, Harry Sutton, chair
- Metropolitan Area Zoo, August 10, 1966, John Mooty, chair
- Refuse Collection and Disposal in the Metropolitan Area, November 23, 1966, John W. Pulver, chair
- Preserving Green Space in Metropolitan Development, July 2, 1968, Clem Springer, chair

- Needed: Better Ways of Making Environmental Choices, January 13, 1971, C. Paul Jones, chair

## Health

- Future Status and Control of Minneapolis General Hospital, March 20, 1963, James R. Pratt, chair
- Hospital Centers . . . And a Health Care System, July 15, 1970, Richard FitzGerald, chair Parks etc

## Housing

- Adequate Housing is Now Everyone's Problem, May 5, 1969, John McGrory, chair
- Better Use of Land and Housing, April 30, 1971, Thomas Beech, chair

## Personnel

- Hennepin County need for a Uniform Merit Personnel System, May 10, 1965, John Pulver, chair
- Another Quiet Crisis: Public Employment, December 18, 1968, Harold D. Field, Jr., chair

## Tax and Finance

- Property Tax Assessment Procedures, April 10, 1963, Willis F. Shaw, chair
- Property Tax Assessment Reform, May 14, 1965, Earl F. Colborn, Jr., chair
- Tax Relief and Reform Proposal (state sales tax), May 5, 1967, David Graven and John Mooty, co-chairs
- Breaking the Tyranny of the Local Property Tax(tax-base sharing), March 20, 1969, Earl F. Colborn, Jr., chair
- New Formulas for Revenue Sharing in Minnesota (school and municipal aid), September 1, 1970, William J. Hempel, chair

## Transportation

- Transportation Problem in the Twin Cities Area, April 7, 1965, James P. Martineau, chair
- Minneapolis Residential Street Paving, June 17, 1966, Norman E. Stewart, chair
- Highways, Transit and the Metropolitan Council, December 6, 1968, John Sullivan, chair
- New Airports for the '70's (And After), October 15, 1969, Waverly Smith, chair
- Transit: The Key Thing to Build is Usage, February 17, 1971, Wayne H. Olson, chair

## Senate recorded vote on final passage of tax-base sharing bill in 1971

On final passage 12 suburban Senators and 19 non-metro Senators voted against the bill. The vote:[311]

Conservatives for (17)—J. T. Anderson, St. Paul; Robert Brown, Stillwater; William Dosland, Moorhead; Kelton Gage, Mankato; Rollin Glewwe, South St. Paul; Mel Hansen, Minneapolis; Stanley Holmquist, Grove City; Roy Holsten, Minneapolis; Keith Hughes, St. Cloud; Glenn McCarty, Minneapolis; William McCutcheon, St. Paul; Harmon Ogdahl, Minneapolis; Joseph O'Neill, St. Paul; Paul Overgaard, Albert Lea; George Pillsbury, Orono; Wayne Popham, Minneapolis, and Cliff Ukkelberg, Clitherall.

DFLers for (17)—Norbert Arnold, Pengilly; Winston Borden, Brainerd; John Chenoweth, St. Paul; Nicholas Coleman, St. Paul; Jack Davies, Minneapolis; Ralph Doty, Duluth; Edward Gearty, Minneapolis; Earl Gustafson, Duluth; N. W. Hanson, Cromwell; J. M. Hughes, Maplewood; Harold Kalina, Minneapolis; Gene Mammenga, Bemidji; Roger Moe, Ada; Edward Novak, St. Paul; Alec Olson, Willmar; Robert Tennessen, Minneapolis, and Myron Wegener, Bertha.

Conservatives against (15)—E. J. Anderson, Frost; Robert Ashbach, Arden Hills; Alf Bergerud, Edina; Jerome Blatz, Bloomington; Mel Fredrick, West Concord; Carl Jensen, Sleepy Eye; J. A. Josefson, Minneota;

William Kirchner, Richfield; Lew Larson, Mabel; John Metcalf, Shakopee; Dean Nyquist, Brooklyn Center; John Olson, Worthington; Richard Palmer, Duluth; Earl Renneke, Le Sueur, and Kenneth Wolfe, St. Louis Park.

DFLers against (16)—J. C. Anderson, North Branch; C. J. Benson, Ortonville; Florian Chmiewlewski, Strugeon Lake; Geroge Conzemius, Cannon Falls; Baldy Hansen, Austin; V. K. Jensen, Montevideo; Victor Jude, Maple Lake; Roger Laufenburger, Lewiston; Howard Olson, St. James; Richard Parish, Golden Valley; A. J. Perpich, Eveleth; George Perpich, Chisholm; Clarence Purfeerst, Faribault; Ed Schrom, Albany; Stanley Thorup, Blaine, and Gerald Willet, Park Rapids.

## House recorded vote on final passage of tax-base sharing bill in 1971

The House vote:[312]

Conservatives for (57)—Salisbury Adams, Orono; Howard Albertson, Stillwater; Richard Andersen, New Brighton; Robert Becklin, Cambridge; Tony Bennett, St. Paul; John Bernhagen, Hutchinson; John Biersdorf, Owatonna; Edward Brandt, Minneapolis; Arne Carlson, Minneapolis; Douglas Carlson, Sandstone; Warren Chamberlain, Faribault; Frank DeGroat, Lake Park; Aubrey Dirlam, Redwood Falls; Robert Dunn, Princeton; Dale Erdahl, Blue Earth; Wendell Erickson, Hills; W. Casper Frischer, Marshall; Richard Fitzsimmons, Warren; Gary Flakne, Minneapolis; Donald Forseth, Crystal; Bertram Fuller, Hayfield; Jon Haven, Alexandria; Roger Hanson, Vergas; Julian Hook, St. Louis Park; George Humphrey, Minneapolis, C. A. Johnson, Mankato; John Johnson, Minneapolis; Ralph Jopp, Mayer; Howard Knutson, Burnsville; Adolph Kvam, Litchfield; Calvin Larson, Fergus Falls; Ernest Lindstrom, Richfield; Verne Long, Pipestone; Sidney Mason, Duluth; M. J. McCauley, Winona; August Mueller, Arlington; Leonard Myrah, Spring Grove; Rolf Nelson, Golden Valley; Tom Newcome, White Bear Lake; Joseph Niehaus, Sauk Center; Vernon Plaisance, Coon Rapids; Harvey Sathre, Adams; Henry Savelkoul, Albert Lea; Roger Scherer, Brooklyn Center; Alfred Schumann, Eyota; Lyall Schwarzkopf, Minneapolis; Rodney Searle, Waseca; Douglas Sillers, Moorhead; Andrew Skaar, Thief River Falls; Arlan Stangeland, Barnesville; Dwight Swanstrom, Duluth; Steven

Szarke, Buffalo; James Ulland, Duluth; Charles Weaver, Anoka; Richard Wigley, Lake Crystal; Raymond Walcott, Minneapolis; and F. Gordon Wright, Minneapolis.

DFLers for (26)—James Adams, Minneapolis; Sam Barr, Ortonville; Thomas Berg, Minneapolis; John Boland, Maplewood; Stanley Enebo, Minneapolis; Raymond Faricy, St. Paul; Stanley Fudro, Minneapolis; Walter Hanson, St. Paul; Jack Kleinbaum, St. Cloud; Donald Moe, St. Paul; Willard Munger, Duluth; Richard Nolan, Little Falls; Robert North, St. Paul; Fred Norton, St. Paul; Richard O'Dea, Mahtomedi; Paul Petrafeso, St. Louis Park; William Quirin, Rochester; Roy Ryan, St. Paul; Martin Sabo, Minneapolis; John Skeate, Minneapolis; Howard Smith, Crosby; Spencer Sokolowski, St. Anthony; Sam Solon, Duluth; Vernon Sommerdorf, St. Paul; James Swanson, Richfield, and Bruce Vento, St. Paul.

Conservatives against (9)—Delbert Anderson, Starbuck; Otto Bang, Edina; Joseph Graw, Bloomington; Thomas Hagedorn, Truman; O. J. Heinitz, Plymouth; John Keefe, Hopkins; R. L. Pavlak, St. Paul; Eugene Smith, Montevideo, and Robert Bell, St. Paul.

DFLers against (30)—Irvin Anderson, International Falls; Bernard Brinkman, Richmond; Bernard Carlson, Coquet; Joseph Connors, Fridley; Robert Culhane, Waterville; Patrick Daugherty, Minneapolis; A. J. Eckstein, New Ulm; Peter Fugina, Virginia; Joseph Graba, Wadena; Neil Haugerud, Preston; C. M. Johnson, St. Peter; Jack Lavoy, Duluth; L. J. Lee, Bagley; Richard Lemke, Lake City; George Mann, Windom; Helen McMillan, Austin; Richard Menke, Prior Lake; William Ojala, Aurora; Raymond Pavlak, South St. Paul; Harry Peterson, Madison; Norman Prahl, Grand Rapids; James Rice, Minneapolis; John Salchert, Minneapolis; Donald Samuelson, Brainerd; Victor Schulz, Goodhue; W. D. Shores, Murdock; Harry Sieben, Hastings; Thomas Simmons, Olivia; Thomas Ticen, Bloomington, and Bill Walker, Pine City.

Abstaining—John Bares, Sauk Rapids.

Excused—Harold Anderson, Minneapolis Conservative; Willis Eken, Twin Valley DFLer; Robert Falk, Tenstrike, DFLer; Jack Fena, Hibbing DFLer; Paul Gerhardt, Fairmont DFLer; Wallace Gustafson, Willmar Conservative; Douglas Johnson, Cook DFLer; Robert W. Johnson, St. Paul Conservative; Francis Judge, Worthington, DFLer; William Kelly, East Grand Forks DFLer; Joseph Prifrel, St. Paul DFLer, and John Wingard, Champlin Conservative.

# Endnotes

1. Myron Orfield and Thomas Luce, " Regional Tax-Base Sharing: A Policy to Promote Fiscal Equity and Efficient Development Practices at the Metropolitan Scale", April 14-15, 2016. https:// socialinnovation.usc.edu/ wp-content/uploads/2017/09/ Orfield-Tax-Base-Sharing-Final.pdf

2. "Air-Rail Chiefs Meet, Outline Line to Chicago", *Minneapolis Star*, August 3, 1928, 4.

3. "Senate OKs Metropolitan Airports Bill", *Minneapolis Star Journal*, April 14, 1943, 1.

4. "Selection of Sewage Plant Site Approved", *Minneapolis Sunday Tribune*, September 14, 1930, 1.

5. "For thirty years, electric streetcars ruled Twin Cities streets", minnpost. com, https://www.minnpost.com/ mnopedia/2016/03/ thirty-years-electric-streetcars-ruled-twin-cities-streets/

6. "Minnesota School Finance History: 1849-2019", Minnesota Department of Education, October 2019, https://webcache. googleusercontent.com/search?q=ca che:Tuj4MSbZr90J:https:// education.mn.gov/mdeprod/ idcplg%3FIdcService%3DGET_ FILE%26dDocName%3D005211%

26RevisionSelectionMethod%3Dlat estReleased%26Rendition%3Dprim ary+&cd=1&hl=en&ct=clnk&gl=us &client=firefox-b-1-d

7. "State Adopts Historic Changes in Policy on Local Government", *Citizens League News*, November 18, 1971.

8. "Minnesota Sales Tax Rates by City", SALE-TAX.COM, July 1, 2020, http://www.sale-tax.com/ Minnesota

9. Charles Tiebout, University of Washington,, "A Pure Theory of Local Expenditures", 1956, https:// en.wikipedia.org/wiki/ Tiebout_model

10. Kenneth T. Jackson, *Crabgrass Frontier: The Suburbanization of the United States.* New York: Oxford University Press, 1985, 142-143.

11. Jackson, "*Crabgrass*", 149.

12. Dr. William P. Marchione, "Annexation Spurned: Brookline's 1873 Rejection of Boston", Brighton Allston Historical Society, http:// www.bahistory.org/ HistoryAnnexBrookline.html

13. Orfield, "Regional Tax-Base Sharing", 2

14. "Predictions Fulfilled", *Minneapolis Tribune*, August 11, 1886, 4.

15. "South St. Paul Folk Oppose Annexation", *Star Tribune,* May 14, 1916, 2.

16. "Annexation Forces Win in Richfield", *Minneapolis Daily Star,* December 8, 1926, p. 1.

17. "History of Richfield, Minnesota", https://en.wikipedia.org/wiki/ Richfield,_Minnesota#History

18. "Columbia Heights Annexation Plans Blocked by Group", *Minneapolis Star,* February 27, 1930, p. 1.

19. "Plan To Annex Robbinsdale is Defeated Again", *Minneapolis Tribune,* December 9, 1931, p. 1.

20. "Cities 101--Consolidations", *National League of Cities,* December 14, 2016, https://www.nlc.org/resource/ cities-101-consolidations

21. *Burnsville '76: A Community History.* Bicentennial Heritage Committee, Burnsville, MN, 1976.

22. Burnsville Historical Society Archives, http://www. burnsvillehistory.org/cpg/ displayimage.php?album=search&c at=0&pid=16380#top_display_ media

23. "Bloomington Moves to Annex 25 Square Miles", *Minneapolis Star,* August 23, 1961, 1.

24. "Burnsville Charts Battle on Bloomington Black Dog Action", *Minneapolis Star,* August 24, 1961,. 1.

25. Bob Ylvisaker, "High Court Denies Black Dog Annexation by Bloomington", *Minneapolis Morning Tribune,* April 25, 1964, 17.

26. "Metropolitan Council 2019 Final Population and Household Estimates", July 2020, https:// metrocouncil.org/Data-and-Maps/ Publications-And-Resources/ Files-and-reports/2019-Population- Estimates-(FINAL,-July-2020).aspx

27. "Burnsville Charts Battle on Bloomington Black Dog Action", *Minneapolis Star,* August 24, 1961,. 1.

28. "NSP Says St. Paul Site Inadequate", *Minneapolis Star,* August 10, 1964, 7A.

29. Carol Honsa, "NSP Power Plant Plans Get St. Croix Opposition," *Minneapolis Star,* July 14, 1964, 1B.

30. Ted Kolderie, "Two Main Factors in St. Croix Dispute Not Involved in Decision", *Minneapolis Star,* December 14, 1964, 12A.

31. "Minutes of Meeting", Metropolitan Fiscal Disparities Committee, Citizens League, March 14, 1968, 2, https://irp-cdn.multiscreensite. com/564352d7/files/uploaded/ Paul%20Gilje%20-%20 Minutes%2C%20Citizens%20 League%20Committee%20031468. pdf

32. "4,000,000 by 2000", the Joint Program, Twin Cities Metropolitan Planning Commission, December 1964, 38.

33. Gwenyth Jones, "MPC Approves Policies to Guide Area Growth," *Minneapolis Star,* July 15, 1966, 7A.

34. "Metropolitan Area Park Needs," Citizens League, December 1964, https://citizensleague.org/ wp-content/uploads/2017/08/ PolicyReportLandDec-54.pdf

35. Ted Kolderie, "Urban Unification Demands Change in Public Finance System", *Minneapolis Star,* October 29, 1965, 14A.

36. "Text of Tax Report to Mayors", *Minneapolis Star,* January 19, 1967, 4B

37. Joe Rigert, "Mayors Unit Urges City Income Tax", *Minneapolis Tribune,* February 14, 1967, 1.

38. "City is 4th Lowest in Land Tax Study", *Minneapolis Star*, February 3, 1967, 12B.

39. Bob Weber, "Side Effects of Tax Move Into Spotlight", *Minneapolis Star*, June 2, 1967, 1.

40. Peter Ackerberg, "LeVander Will Sign Metro Unit Bill Tuesday", *Minneapolis Star*, May 20, 1967, 1.

41. Peter Ackerberg, "Campaign Launched for Reorganization of Area Tax Power", *Minneapolis Star*, December 8, 1967, 1.

42. Ted Kolderie, "Metropolitan Reorganization: The Fiscal Side", Upper Midwest Research and Development Council, December 1967, 2, https://irp-cdn. multiscreensite.com/564352d7/files/ uploaded/St.%20Thomas%20 Conference%20discussion%20 paper%20120867.pdf

43. Kolderie, "Metropolitan Reorganization" 9-10.

44. Marvin McNeff, "Ham Lake Airport Site Proposed", *Minneapolis Star*, April 23, 1968, 2C.

45. Peter Ackerberg, "Ham Lake Veto a 'Mickey Finn' Backers Charge, *Minneapolis Star*, April 25, 1969, 1.

46. "Predictions Fulfilled", *Minneapolis Tribune*, August 11, 1886, 4.

47. F. Warren Preeshl, "A suggestion for an areawide uniform tax levy on total business and commercial property in the seven county metropolitan area for school district and municipal purposes," June 14, 1968, 1, https://irp-cdn. multiscreensite.com/564352d7/files/ uploaded/Paul%20Gilje%20-%20 Original%20Preeshal%20 memo%20on%20TBS%20061468. pdf

48. Minutes of Meeting, Citizens League Metropolitan Fiscal Disparities Committee, December 12, 1968, 3, https://irp-cdn. multiscreensite.com/564352d7/files/ uploaded/Paul%20Gilje%20-%20 Minutes%2C%20Fiscal%20 Disparities%20Committee%20 121268.pdf

49. Kaye Rakow and Bob DeBoer, "How Fiscal Disparities Spreads Property Tax Base Around the Region", NAIOP Minnesota Chapter, https://citizensleague.org/ wp-content/uploads/2017/08/ PropertyTaxFiscalDisparities- Sharing-Wealth.pdf

50. "Minutes of Meeting", Citizens League Board of Directors, September 27, 1967, 3, https:// irp-cdn.multiscreensite. com/564352d7/files/uploaded/ Paul%20Gilje%20-%20 Minutes%20Board%20032069.pdf

51. Paul Gilje, "Preliminary List of Possible Research and Action Projects" Citizens League, June 11, 1965, 1, https://irp-cdn. multiscreensite.com/564352d7/files/ uploaded/Paul%20Gilje%20-%20 Early%20mention%20of%20 possible%20disparities%20 project%20061165.pdf

52. "Breaking the Tyranny of the Local Property Tax", Citizens League, March 20, 1969, 30, https:// citizensleague.org/wp-content/ uploads/2017/08/ PolicyReportFiscalMarch-69.pdf

53. "Minutes of Meeting", Metropolitan Fiscal Disparities Committee, Citizens League, March 7, 1968, https://irp-cdn.multiscreensite. com/564352d7/files/uploaded/ Paul%20Gilje%20-%20 Minutes%20Fiscal%20 Disparities%20Committee%20 030768.pdf

54. "Minutes of Meeting", Metropolitan Fiscal Disparities Committee, Citizens League, March 14, 1968, https://irp-cdn.multiscreensite.com/564352d7/files/uploaded/Paul%20Gilje%20-%20Minutes%2C%20Citizens%20League%20Committee%20031468.pdf

55. "Minutes of Meeting", Metropolitan Fiscal Disparities Committee, Citizens League, March 28, 1968, https://irp-cdn.multiscreensite.com/564352d7/files/uploaded/Paul%20Gilje%20-%20Minutes%2C%20Fiscal%20Disparities%20Committee%2C%20032868.pdf

56. "Minutes of Meeting", Metropolitan Fiscal Disparities Committee, Citizens League, July 25, 1968, https://irp-cdn.multiscreensite.com/564352d7/files/uploaded/Paul%20Gilje%20-%20Minutes%2C%20Fiscal%20Disparities%20Committee%2C%20072568.pdf

57. "Fiscal Disparities-Related Data", Staff Memo, Metropolitan Fiscal Disparities Committee, Citizens League, March 21, 1968, https://irp-cdn.multiscreensite.com/564352d7/files/uploaded/Paul%20Gilje%20-%20Fiscal%20Disparities-related%20data%20032168.pdf

58. George McCormick, "Where You Live Makes a Tax Difference," *Minneapolis Tribune*, February 2, 1969, 7B.

59. "Proposals for Reducing Property Tax Differences in the Metropolitan Area", Metropolitan Fiscal Disparities Committee, Citizens League, December 26, 1968, https://irp-cdn.multiscreensite.com/564352d7/files/uploaded/Paul%20Gilje%20-%20CL%20memo%20outlining%20disparities%20proposals%20122668.pdf

60. "Minutes of Meetings", Metropolitan Fiscal Disparities Committee, Citizens League, December 12, 1968, https://irp-cdn.multiscreensite.com/564352d7/files/uploaded/Paul%20Gilje%20-%20Minutes%2C%20Fiscal%20Disparities%20Committee%20121268.pdf; January 2, 1969, https://irp-cdn.multiscreensite.com/564352d7/files/uploaded/Paul%20Gilje%20-%20Disp%20minutes%20010269.pdf; January 16, 1969, https://irp-cdn.multiscreensite.com/564352d7/files/uploaded/Paul%20Gilje%20-%20Disp%20minutes%20011669.pdf; January 23, 1969, https://irp-cdn.multiscreensite.com/564352d7/files/uploaded/Paul%20Gilje%20-%20Disp%20minutes%20012369.pdf

61. "Minutes of Meetings".

62. "Breaking the Tyranny of the Local Property Tax", 2.

63. "Minutes of Meetings", Board of Directors, Citizens League, March 5, 1969, https://irp-cdn.multiscreensite.com/564352d7/files/uploaded/Paul%20Gilje%20-%20Minutes%20Board%20030569.pdf; March 14, 1969, https://irp-cdn.multiscreensite.com/564352d7/files/uploaded/Paul%20Gilje%20-%20Minutes%20Board%20031469.pdf; March 20, 1969, https://irp-cdn.multiscreensite.com/564352d7/files/uploaded/board%20oks%20colborn%20report%20032069.pdf

64. "Economist Francis Boddy dies at 76", *Minneapolis Star and Tribune*, March 21, 1983, 8B.

65. Robert L. Ehlers, "Minority Committee Report of the Fiscal Disparities Committee", Citizens League, March 14, 1969, https://citizensleague.org/wp-content/uploads/2017/08/PolicyReportFiscalMarch-69-2.pdf

66. Ted Kolderie, "Existing Fiscal Policy, the Consequences, New Objectives...And a Challenge", Citizens League, 1969, https://irp-cdn.multiscreensite.com/564352d7/files/uploaded/Paul%20Gilje%20-%20Existing%20Fiscal%20Policy%20Kolderie%20display%201969.pdf; Kolderie, Ted, "Growth-of-the-Area Plan", Citizens League, 1969, https://irp-cdn.multiscreensite.com/564352d7/files/uploaded/Paul%20Gilje%20-%20GOTA%20plan%20w%20Kolderie%20notes%201968.pdf

67. Bernie Shellum, "Citizens Group Urges 7-County Tax Pool", *Minneapolis Tribune*, March 27, 1969, 1.

68. Paul Gilje, "New South High Urged to Displace Central", *Minneapolis Star*, October 28, 1963, 1.

69. Myron Orfield and Nicholas Wallace, *The Minnesota Fiscal Disparities Act of 1971*, 33 Wm. Mitchell L. Rev. 591, 2007, *available at* https://scholarship.law.umn.edu/imo_studies/60/

70. Ted Kolderie, *Thinking Out the How*, Beaver's Pond Press, 2017, 86-89.

71. Myron Orfield, *Metropolitics A Regional Agenda for Community and Stability*, The Brookings Institution, 1997, 143-144

72. "Metro Base-Sharing Plan Approved by Legislature", July 1971 *Citizens League News*

73. Tom Berg, *Minnesota's Miracle: Learning from the Government that Worked*, University of Minnesota Press, Minneapolis, 2012.

74. Alan Dale Albert, "Sharing Suburbia's Wealth: The Political Economy of Tax Base Sharing in Minnesota's Twin Cities Metropolitan Area", Harvard College, March 1979.

75. Albert, 94-95.

76. Albert, 95-96.

77. Albert, 97. Weaver's letter is similar to Preeshl's proposal, which had been drafted five months earlier. One wonders whether Weaver might have spoken with Preeshl before writing the letter. But there's no evidence of such a conversation.

78. Albert, 98-99.

79. "Bloomington Wants Property-Tax Study", *Minneapolis Star*, January 23, 1969, 11B.

80. Albert, 100.

81. Albert, 118.

82. Albert, 101.

83. Albert, 101.

84. Albert, 102.

85. Albert, 102.

86. "House Backs Tax Sharing in Metro Area", *Minneapolis Tribune*, May 16, 1969, 12.

87. Albert, 103.

88. Albert, 103.

89. "House Backs Tax Sharing in Metro Area", *Minneapolis Tribune*, May 16, 1969, 12.

90. Albert, 104-105.

91. Kolderie, "Thinking Out the How"

92. Albert, 105.

93. Citizens League *News*, April 18, 1969, 1.

94. Albert, 106-107.

95. Albert, 109-110

96. Albert, 111.

97. Albert, 112.

98. "House passes bill to share part of future regional tax-base hike," *Minneapolis Star*, April 1, 1971, 9A.

99. Orfield, *Metropolitics*, 143.

100. Albert, 112-113.

101. Albert, 113.

102. Albert, 115.

103. Albert, 116.

104. Albert, 119.

105. Albert, 120.

106. Steven Dornfeld, "Senate unit backs tax-sharing", *Minneapolis Tribune*, May 6, 1971, 1B.

107. Albert, 120-121.

108. Albert, 121-122.

109. Albert, 122.

110. Albert, 123.

111. Albert, 123.

112. Albert, 124.

113. Deborah Howell, "'Disparities' bill in trouble?", *Minneapolis Star*, July 13, 1971, 6A.

114. Albert, 124. Albert's words, "every House Conservative" are intended to mean "every House Conservative who voted for the bill in the regular session."

115. Editorial, "DFL and fiscal disparities", *Minneapolis Tribune*, July 14, 1971, 14A.

116. Albert, 125.

117. Finlay Lewis, "Metro area to pool tax base under new law, *Minneapolis Tribune*, July 16, 1971, 1A.

118. Albert 125.

119. Albert, 126.

120. Albert, 126.

121. Albert, 127.

122. Jared Swanson and Steve Hinze, "Minnesota's Fiscal Disparities Law", February 2020, https://www.house.leg.state.mn.us/hrd/pubs/fiscaldis.pdf, 3-10.

123. "New Formulas for Revenue Sharing in Minnesota", Citizens League, September 1, 1970, https://citizensleague.org/wp-content/uploads/2017/08/PolicyReportFiscalSept-70.pdf

124. Ted Smebakken, "Anderson for 100% state school aid", *Minneapolis Star*, October 2, 1970, 1A

125. "The Crisis Continues", 13th Annual Report, Advisory Commission on Intergovernmental Relations, February 1972, https://library.unt.edu/gpo/acir/Reports/information/M-73.pdf, 5.

126. "Can't-Miss Play: Stefon Diggs' Minnesota Miracle Catch", January 14, 2018, https://www.nfl.com/videos/can-t-miss-play-stefon-diggs-minnesota-miracle-catch-286256

127. "The Crisis Continues", 6.

128. "State Adopts Historic Changes in Policy on Local Government", *Citizens League News*, November 18, 1971.

129. Editorial, "In tax-base sharing, it's the 'losers' that win", *Minneapolis Star and Tribune*, November 4, 1983, 14A.

130. Tracy Gordon, "Critics Argue The Property Tax Is Unfair. Do They Have A Point?", Tax Policy Center and Brookings Institution, March 9, 2020, https://www.taxpolicycenter.org/taxvox/critics-argue-property-tax-unfair-do-they-have-point

131. Betty Wilson, "Area auditors to get property tax guidelines", *Minneapolis Star*, September 13, 1974, 5A.

132. Wilson, 5A.

133. Betty Wilson, "Law spreads metro-area expansion of tax base", *Minneapolis Star*, January 17, 1975, 1A.

134. Swanson and Hinze, 7.

135. "County Auditor's Steps in Base Sharing", Citizens League, September 21, 1971, https://irp-cdn.multiscreensite.com/564352d7/files/uploaded/Paul%20Gilje%20-%20County%20Auditor%27s%20steps%20in%20TBS%20Nov.%201971.pdf

Administrative Auditor's Responsibilities", Citizens League, September 21, 1971, https://irp-cdn.multiscreensite.com/564352d7/files/uploaded/Paul%20Gilje%20-%20Administrative%20Auditor%27s%20responsiblities%20112171.pdf

136. Betty Wilson, "Burnsville to test 'fiscal disparities' law", *Minneapolis Star*, March 8, 1972, 1.

137. Wilson, "Burnsville to test", 1.

138. Betty Wlson, "Tax-sharing appeal all Burnsville's", *Minneapolis Star*, March 14,1972, 4A.

139. Editorial, "An all-American area?" *Minneapolis Tribune*, March 11, 1972, 4A.

140. "Robert Breunig, retired judge, dies at 66", *Minneapolis Tribune*, February 9, 1990, 6B.

141. Quoted in Village of Burnsville v. Onischuk, 301 Minn. 137, 222 N.W. 2nd 523 (1974)

142. Betty Wilson, "Burnsville maverick on more than tax law", *Minneapolis Star*, February 1, 1973, 1B

143. Betty Wilson, "Tax-sharing case, suit against airport heard", *Minneapolis Star*, September 29, 1973, 11A.

144. "Amicus Curiae: The Citizens League", Village of Burnsville v. Onischuk. (File Nos. 44232, 44253, Minn. Sup. Ct.) //mn.gov/law-library-stat/briefs/pdfs/222NW2d523ac1.pdf

145. "Amicus Curiae: The City of Bloomington", Village of Burnsville v. Onischuk (File Nos. 44232, 44253, Minn. Sup. Ct.) //mn.gov/law-library-stat/briefs/pdfs/222NW2d523ac2.pdf

146. "Disparity law requires sharing of 'new' tax base" *Minneapolis Star*, September 13, 1974, 7B.

147. Village of Burnsville v. Onischuk, 301 Minn. 137, 222 N.W.2d 523 (1974).

148. "Disparity law requires sharing of 'new' tax base"

149. "Supreme Court refuses review of state's fiscal disparities law", *Minneapolis Star*, February 21, 1975, p. 9. 420 U.S. 916 (1975).

150. Dan Wascoe, Jr. "Mayor to leave his mark on Burnsville," *Minneapolis Tribune*, November 24, 1975, 1A.

151. John W. Windhorst, Jr., "The Minnesota Fiscal Disparities Law", July 1, 1975, 9, https://irp-cdn.multiscreensite.com/564352d7/files/uploaded/Paul%20Gilje%20-%20John%20W.%20Windhorst%2C%20Jr.%20analysis%20of%20TBS%20070175.pdf

152. "Shakopee MN Demographics", https://www.shakopeemn.gov/living-here/about-shakopee/demographics

153. McCutcheon v. State, Nos. TC-123,124 & 125 (Minn. T.C., Feb. 12, 1981).

154. Paul Gilje, "Shakopee appeal of tax-base sharing law", Citizens League, May 20, 1981, https://

irp-cdn.multiscreensite.
com/564352d7/files/uploaded/
Paul%20Gilje%20-%20
Shakopee%20appeal%20052081.
pdf

155. Amicus Curiae: The Citizens
League, "McCutcheon v. State (File
No. 81-368, Minn. Sup. Ct)",
https://citizensleague.org/
wp-content/uploads/2017/08/
PolicyReportFiscal1981-1.pdf, 17.

156. *McCutcheon v. State*, **No. 81-368
(Minn. Feb. 19, 1982)**.

157. Walker v. Itasca County Auditor,
624 N.W.2d 599 (Minn. App. 2001).

158. Walker v. Itasca County Auditor,
642 N.W.2d 745 (Minn. 2002).

159. San Antonio Indep. Sch. Dist. v.
Rodriguez, 411 U. S. 1, 40-41

160. Erick Trickey, "Why the Colonies'
Most Galvanizing Patriot Never
Became a Founding Father",
*Smithsonian Magazine,* May 5, 2017,
https://www.smithsonianmag.com/
history/
transformative-patriot-who-didnt-
become-founding-
father-180963166/

161. "James C. Otis, Associate Justice
1961-1982", Minnesota State Law
Library, https://mncourts.libguides.
com/otis

162. Betty Wilson, "Legislators seek tax
'equalizer' repeal", *Minneapolis Star,*
January 25, 1975, 7A.

163. "The 1979 Minnesota
Tax-Increment Financing Act,"
*William Mitchell Law Review*: Vol. 7 :
Iss. 3 , Article 2, https://open.
mitchellhamline.edu/wmlr/vol7/
iss3/2, 632-633.

164. "The 1979 Minnesota…", 659.

165. Paul Gilje, "Metropolitan tax-base
sharing and tax-increment financing
in development districts", Citizens

League, September 27, 1978,
https://irp-cdn.multiscreensite.
com/564352d7/files/uploaded/
Paul%20Gilje%20-%20
Tax-base%20sharing%20and%20
TIF%20092778.pdf

166. Swanson and Hinze, 5.

167. Robert Guenther, "'Cinderella'
areas rise through ashes of blight",
*Minneapolis Star,* July 5, 1978, 1A.

168. "Tax Increment Financing
Legislative Report", Office of the
State Auditor, March 5, 2020,
http://www.osa.state.mn.us/
reports/tif/2018/tifLegislative/
tifLegislative_18_report.pdf, i.

169. Lori Sturdevant, "Legislature
approves stadium bill", *Minneapolis
Tribune,* May 22, 1979, 1.

170. Ralph Vartabedian, "Twin Cities
get CAB nod for London route",
*Minneapolis Star,* January 25, 1980,
2D.

171. Paul Gustafson, "City officials
fishing for draw card in plans to
redevelop stadium site," *Minneapolis
Star,* October 1, 1981, 10 south.

172. Ellen Foley, "Stadium impact study
has potential for feud", *Minneapolis
Star and Tribune,* July 28, 1983, 5 lake.

173. Editorial, "How not to pay for a
convention center", *Minneapolis Star
and Tribune,* August 3, 1984, 12A.

174. Wendy S. Tai, "$1 billion Met
Stadium plan OK'd", *Minneapolis
Star and Tribune,* July 3, 1985, 1.

175. "Best in retail, entertainment and
attractions", Mall of America,
https://www.mallofamerica.com/
about#

176. Tai, "$1 billion…",13A

177. Editorial, "Movement on the
convention-center front", *Minneapolis
Star and Tribune,* August 1, 1985, 16A.

178. Paul Gilje, "Property tax/fiscal disparities options for financing Triple Five project in Bloomington", Community Information Committee, Citizens League, August 8, 1985, https://irp-cdn. multiscreensite.com/564352d7/files/ uploaded/Paul%20Gilje%20-%20 Megamall%20TBS%20options%20 %20internal%20memo%20CL%20 081585%20%20%20%20%20%20 %20%20%20%20%20%20%20 %20%20%20%20%20%20%20 %20%20%20%20%20%20%20 %20%20%20%20%20%2085.pdf

179. "Statement to House Tax Subcommittee on Fiscal Disparities", Citizens League, October 31, 1985, https:// citizensleague.org/wp-content/ uploads/2017/08/ PolicyReportFiscalOct-85-1.pdf

180. Gregor W. Pinney, "Work on subsidy request stalls mega-mall lobbying", *Minneapolis Star and Tribune*, January 26, 1986, 15A.

181. Wendy S. Tai and Gregor W. Pinney, "Mega-mall's future appears uncertain; backers are bitter", *Minneapolis Star and Tribune*, March 30, 1986, 1A.

182. Gregor W. Pinney and Wendy S. Tai, "Mall could have 800 stores, says Ghermezian", *Minneapolis Star and Tribune*, May 7, 1986, 1A.

183. Editorial, "How not to 'save' fiscal disparities", *Star Tribune*, March 15, 1988, 10.

184. "Statement on Changing the Fiscal Disparities Law", Citizens League, January 15, 1988, https:// citizensleague.org/wp-content/ uploads/2017/08/ PolicyReportFiscalJan-88.pdf

185. Swanson and Hinze.

186. Jeff Spartz, "Fiscal-disparities law", Letters from readers, *Star Tribune*, December 7, 1987, 14A.

187. John Rajkowski, "County board is fed up with the inequity of fiscal disparities", *St. Louis Park Sailor*, February 5, 1988, 2A.

188. Charles R. Weaver, "In defense of fiscal disparities Commentary/ Counterpoint, *Star Tribune*, March 25, 1989, 11A.

189. Jeff Spartz, "Disparities law needs reform", Commentary/ Counterpoint, *Star Tribune*, May 6, 1989, 21A.

190. Jeff Spartz, "The Monday Briefing/ Government, Verbatim", *Star Tribune*, January 1, 1990, 3B

191. Norman Draper, "Hennepin wants share-the-wealth program changed", *Star Tribune*, January 22, 1991, 3B.

192. Editorial, "It's beggar-thy-metro-neighbor time again", *Star Tribune*, January 23, 1991, 16A.

193. Peter McLaughlin and John Keefe, "20-year-old fiscal-disparities program is riddled with inequities", Commentary/Counterpoint, *Star Tribune*, March 9,m 1991, 13A.

194. Charlie Weaver (son of Charles R. Weaver) and other state representatives, letter to Governor Arne Carlson, March 6, 1991 https://irp-cdn.multiscreensite. com/564352d7/files/ uploaded/1991%20Charlie%20 Weaver%20to%20Gov%20 Carlson%20urging%20no%20 changes%20in%20TBS.pdf,

195. Editorial, "Fend off latest attack on metro-area sharing", *St. Paul Pioneer Press*, March 12, 1991.

196. Mary E. Anderson, "Let's keep sharing benefits of growth", *Metro Monitor*, Metropolitan Council , March-April 1991, 2.

197. Charlie Weaver, "County Board's plan would take from poor, give to rich", Commentary/Counterpoint, *Star Tribune*, March 23, 1991, 15A.

198. Swanson and Hinze, 22-23.

199. Orfield, *Metropolitics:*, 55.

200. Dane Smith, "Bill seeks to balance metro growth with opportunities, *Star Tribune*, February 19, 1993, 3B.

201. Dane Smith, "Transit service turned over to Met Council, *Star Tribune*, May 6, 1994, 1B.

202. Editorial, "He's back! Orfield stays tough on fair housing", *Star Tribune*, March 4, 1994, 20A.

203. Myron Orfield, "Defenders of the status quo ignore a growing regional crisis", *Star Tribune*, March 19,1994, 19

204. Dane Smith, "House backs tax-sharing proposal", *Star Tribune*, May 5, 1995, 1A

205. Steve Brandt, "Met Council may revive housing plan", *Star Tribune*, June 5, 1994, 2B.

206. Mike Kaszuba, "Suburbs clashing over Orfield proposal", *Star Tribune*, March 11, 1995, 1A.

207. Dane Smith, "Ventura's on-air apology not enough for Orfield after 'communist' remark", *Star Tribune*, May 17, 1995, 1B.

208. Swanson and Hinze, 23.

209. "2018 Metropolitan Livable Communities Fund Annual Report", Metropolitan Council, August 2019, https://metrocouncil.org/ Communities/Services/Livable-Communities-Grants/LCA/2017-Livable-Communities-Annual-Report-(pdf).aspx

210. Bob DeBoer, "A new look at fiscal disparities: is it subsidizing development that counters regional

thinking?", Citizens League, *Minnesota Journal*, March 23, 2004, 4.

211. David Peterson, "Fiscal sharing statue panned", *Star Tribune*, March 25, 2004, B1.

212. MN Stat 473f.01(2019), https://law. justia.com/codes/minnesota/2019/ chapters-473-473j/chapter-473f/ section-473f-01/

213. Dee Long, "Conclusions didn't come from League", Counterpoint, *Star Tribune*, April 10, 2004, A17

214. Myron Orfield and Thomas F. Luce, Jr. *Region: Planning the Future of the Twin Cities.* University of Minnesota Press: Minneapolis, MN, 2010, 266.

215. Orfield and Luce, *Region*, 242.

216. Swanson and Hinze, 26.

217. Swanson and Hinze, 26.

218. "Iron Range Fiscal Disparities Study", Property Tax Division, Minnesota Deparment of Revenue, January 31, 2014, https://www. revenue.state.mn.us/sites/default/ files/2018-11/iron_range_fiscal_ disparities_study.pdf

219. Swanson and Hinze, 29.

220. Pam Louwagie, "Appeals Court upholds tax-sharing act for Range," *Star Tribune*, April 11, 2001, B9.

221. Dennis J. McGrath, "Iron Range league rejects revenue sharing proposal", *Star Tribune*, January 14, 1988, 6B.

222. Orfield, *Metropolitics*, 155.

223. "Base-sharing Impact is As Legislature Intended", *Citizens League News*, January 31, 1975, 1.

224. "Tax-base sharing raw data for metro area, 2020", House Research, https://irp-cdn.multiscreensite. com/564352d7/files/uploaded/ Paul%20A.%20Gilje%20-%20 Copy%20of%20FDDataPay20-GiljeCorr3.pdf

225. "Tax-Base Sharing is Reducing Differences in Local Valuations, *Citizens League News*, March 19, 1976, 1.

226. "Metropolitan Council 2019 Final Population and Household Estimates", July 2020, https://metrocouncil.org/Data-and-Maps/Publications-And-Resources/Files-and-reports/2019-Population-Estimates-(FINAL,-July-2020).aspx

227. "Welcome to Minnesota House Research Department", https://www.house.leg.state.mn.us/hrd/hrd.aspx

228. Swanson and Hinze, 24.

229. "Fiscal Disparities Free List" , Metropolitan Fiscal Disparities Committee, Citizens League, 1968, https://irp-cdn.multiscreensite.com/564352d7/files/uploaded/Paul%20Gilje%20-%20Free%20list%20Fiscal%20Disparities%20Committee%201968.pdf

230. Minutes of Meeting, Citizens League Metropolitan Fiscal Disparities Committee, December 12, 1968, 1, https://irp-cdn.multiscreensite.com/564352d7/files/uploaded/Paul%20Gilje%20-%20Minutes%2C%20Fiscal%20Disparities%20Committee%20121268.pdf

231. Charles R. Weaver, "Breaking the Tyranny of the Local Property Tax", Proceedings of the Annual Conference on Taxation under the Auspices of the National Tax Association Vol. 63 (1970), pp. 207-222.

232. "Editorial Comment", *National Civic Review*, National Municipal League, September 1971, 425.

233. Editorial, "Good Example from Minnesota", *Milwaukee Journal*, July 24, 1971.

234. Editorial, "The state and metropolitan problems", *Minneapolis Tribune*, July 18, 1971, 14A

235. Katharine C. Lyall, "Tax Base-Sharing: A Fiscal Aid Towards More Rational Land Use Planning", *Journal of the American Institute of Planners*, Vol. 41:2, 1975, p. 90-100.

236. Roy Bahl, "Regional Tax Base Sharing Possibilities and implications", *National Tax Journal*, 1 September 1976, 328-335.

237. Walter H. Plosila, "Metropolitan Tax-Base-Sharing: Its Potential and Limitations", *Public Finance Quarterly*, Vol. 4, p.205, 1976.

238. Andrew Reschovsky and Gene Knaff, "Tax Base Sharing: An assessment of the Minnesota Experience", *Journal of the American Institute of Planners*, Vol. 43:4, 1977, p. 361-370.

239. Paul Smith, "Tax Base Sharing: Local Response to Fiscal Federalism", *Lincoln Institute of Land Policy*, Cambridge, MA, 1979.

240. Walter Vogt, "Tax Base Sharing: Implications from San Diego County", *Journal of the American Planning Association*, Vol. 45:2, 1979, p. 134-142

241. D. A. Gilbert, "Property Tax Base Sharing: An Answer to Central City Fiscal Problems?" *Social Science Quarterly*, Vol. 59, 1979, 68.

242. Andrew Reschovsky, "An Evaluation of Metropolitan Area Tax Base Sharing", *National Tax Journal*, Vol. XXXIII:1, 1980, 55-66.

243. Chris Serres, "Tax bill subsidizes megamall expansion", *Star Tribune*, May 23, 2007, D1.

244. Mark Brunswick, "Pawlenty vetoes tax bill (and more)", *Star Tribune*, May 31, 2007, A1

245. Susan Feyder, "New pitch for aid to mall", *Star Tribune*, March 6, 2008, D1.

246. Feyder, D5.

247. Bob DeBoer, "Testimony on Senate File 1950", Citizens League, March 26, 2008, https://citizensleague.org/wp-content/uploads/2017/08/PolicyReportFiscalMarch-2008.pdf

248. Pat Doyle, "A bigger mall may have to rely on local tax increases", *Star Tribune*, May 19, 2008, B3.

249. Doyle, B3

250. "Study of the Metropolitan Area Fiscal Disparities Program", Tischler/Bise, Bethesda, MD, February 13, 2012, https://www.revenue.state.mn.us/sites/default/files/2018-11/fiscal-disparities-study-full-report.pdf

251. "Study..." Tischler/Bise, 154

252. "Study..." Tischler/Bise, 172

253. "Study..." Tischler/Bise, 174

254. "Study..." Tischler/Bise, 172

255. David Peterson and Katie Humphrey and Laurie Blake, "Tax-share program receives scrutiny", *Star Tribune*, January 31, 2012, 1.

256. Laurie Blake, "Tax-sharing plan's pluses, minuses", *Star Tribune*, February 16, 2012, B5.

257. Bob DeBoer, "House and Senate tax bills misuse 'fiscal disparities'", Opinion, *St. Paul Pioneer Press*, May 10, 2013, 16A.

258. [2]57Bob Doer, "Before altering tax-base pool, let's reflect," Opinion Exchange, *Star Tribune*, May 1 3, 2013, A11.

259. Tom Webb, "MOA hopes tax break jump-starts $1.5B expansion", *St. Paul Pioneer Press*, May 22, 2013, 1A

260. Janet Moore, "MOA nets up to $150M in breaks", *Star Tribune*, May 22, 2013, D1.

261. Steven Dornfeld, "New tax bill laced with special tax breaks for selected businesses, *Minnpost*, May 28, 2013, https://www.minnpost.com/politics-policy/2013/05/new-tax-bill-laced-special-tax-breaks-selected-businesses/

262. "State assistance for Mall of America expansion will prove beneficial to region", Interview, Civic Caucus, May 4, 2014, http://www.civiccaucus.org/discussions/2014/Bloomington-Officials_05-04-14.html

263. Jonathan Wolman, Associated Press, "Suburbs, central cities 'friends again'", *Fort Worth Star-Telegram*, June 23, 1977, 2.

264. Bolton Schwartz, "Authority moves to build complex", Passaic, NJ, *Hearld-News*, May 16, 1972, 17.

265. Robert Ceberio and Ron Kase, "New Jersey Meadowlands A History", The History Press, Charleston, SC, 2015.

266. Roger Lane, "Milliken Plan to Aid Detroit Causes Split", *Detroit Free Press*, January 16, 1976, 1.

267. Luther Jackson, "Tax-base sharing could ease core-city problems", *Detroit Free Press*, March 9, 1987, 1C.

268. Myron Orfield, "Where sharing the tax base works well", *Sacramento Bee*, January 20, 2002, L1.

269. Editorial, "Sales tax sharing: Give regional cooperation a chance", *Sacramento Bee*, January 20, 2002, L4.

270. Karen Brandon, "Sacramento plan shares tax bases to lessen sprawl," *Chicago Tribune*, May 1, 2002, 8.

271. Richard S. Davis, "How Iowa's communities can help each other

develop", Opinion, *Des Moines Register*, December 28, 1984, 7A.

272. "Area development group advocates sharing of taxes," *Des Moines Register*, March 22, 1985, 2M.

273. Jane Norman, "Local officials examine tax-base sharing pros, cons", *Des Moines Register,* September 18, 1985, 3M.

274. Editorial, "The Twin Cities Experience," *The Hartford Courant*, January 27, 2002, C2.

275. Editorial, "Valley of decision", *Pittsburgh Post-Gazette*, March 28, 1988, 12.

276. Forum, "Together we grow", *Pittsburgh Post-Gazette,* April 14, 1996, C-4

277. Tom Murphy, "Tom Murphy", *Pittsburgh Post-Gazette*, June 6, 1999, H-4.

278. "What is RAD?", Allegheny Regional Asset District, https://www.radworkshere.org/pages/how-rad-works

279. Frank Reeves, "In Twin Cities tax-sharing gives everyone slice of development pie", *Pittsburgh Post-Gazette,* February 13, 2004, D-1.

280. Andrew Conte, "Leaders book Twin Cities trip", *TRIBlive*, April 30, 2004, https://archive.triblive.com/news/leaders-book-twin-cities-trip/

281. CONNECT, Congress of Neighboring Communities, University of Pittsburgh, https://gspia.pitt.edu/CentersandInstitutes/Initiatives/CONNECT

282. Young Kim, "Partnership tells local governments to share", *The Morning Call* (Allentown, PA), November 10, 1999, B2.

283. Daryl Nerl, "Spread wealth to cities, Senators told", *The Morning Call*, April 14, 2000, B2.

284. "About GFOA", Government Finance Officers Association, https://www.gfoa.org/about

285. Shayne Kavanagh, "GFOA Study of Government Fragmentation", Government Finance Officers Association, April 26, 2020, https://irp-cdn.multiscreensite.com/564352d7/files/uploaded/2020%20GFOA%20Govt%20Fragmentation%20Summary%20Memo.pdf

286. "Why Not Buy Service?", Citizens League, September 1972, https://citizensleague.org/wp-content/uploads/2017/08/PolicyReportGovernmentSept-72.pdf

287. "Overcoming Obstacles to the Purchase of Service, Citizens League, January 14, 1974, https://citizensleague.org/wp-content/uploads/2017/08/PolicyReportGovernmentJan-74.pdf

288. Paul Smith.

289. John M. Rogers and Steve Hembley, "Regional Economic Development Alliances", Ohio House of Representatives, June 11, 2020, https://www.legislature.ohio.gov/legislation/legislation-summary?id=GA133-HB-631

290. Myron Orfield and Thomas Luce, "NE Ohio-Cleveland Metropatterns", Institute on Metropolitan Opportunity, University of Minnesota Law School, 2008, https://scholarship.law.umn.edu/cgi/viewcontent.cgi?article=1024&context=imo_studies

291. Peter Krouse, "What can Minnesota teach us about sharing?, cleveland.com, September 24, 2019, https://www.cleveland.com/

news/2019/09/what-can-minnesota-teach-us-about-sharing-cleveland-2030-a-way-forward.html

292. Peter Krouse, "Tax sharing in Minnesota means sharing tax base", cleveland.com, September 16, 2019, https://www.cleveland.com/news/2019/09/tax-sharing-in-minnesota-means-sharing-tax-base-cleveland-2030-a-way-forward.html

293. Peter Krouse, "Twin Cities tax sharing creates winners and lowers--or maybe everybody wins", cleveland.com, September 17, 2019, https://www.cleveland.com/news/2019/09/twin-cities-tax-sharing-creates-winners-and-losers-or-maybe-everybody-wins-cleveland-2030-a-way-forward.html

294. Peter Krouse, "The Twin Cities success story began before tax sharing", cleveland.com, September 18, 2019, https://www.cleveland.com/news/2019/09/the-twin-cities-have-embraced-regional-planning-for-more-than-50-years-cleveland-2030-a-way-forward.html

295. Peter Krouse, "Liberals and conservatives embraced tax sharing in the Twin Cities", cleveland.com, September 19, 2019, https://www.cleveland.com/news/2019/09/liberals-and-conservatives-embraced-tax-sharing-in-the-twin-cities-cleveland-2030-a-way-forward.html

296. Peter Krouse, "Twin Cities tax sharing inspires progressive minds here", cleveland.com, September 20, 2019, https://www.cleveland.com/news/2019/09/twin-cities-tax-sharing-inspires-progressive-minds-here-cleveland-2030-a-way-forward.html

297. Peter Krouse, "Peer cities offer Cleveland ideas for an inclusive economy", cleveland.com, December 26, 2019, https://www.cleveland.com/news/2019/12/peer-cities-offer-cleveland-ideas-for-an-inclusive-economy-cleveland-2030-a-way-forward.html

298. Peter Krouse, "Cleveland Rising groups use Zoom meeting to update public on bold ideas for transforming Cleveland", cleveland.com, May 30, 2020, https://www.cleveland.com/news/2020/05/cleveland-rising-groups-use-zoom-meeting-to-update-public-on-bold-ideas-for-transforming-cleveland.html

299. "The Citizens League Itself", *National Civic Review*, National Municipal League, July 1976, https://citizensleague.org/wp-content/uploads/2017/08/PolicyReportPublicPolicyJuly-76.pdf

300. "Priority Issues/Choices Facing Minnesotans", Civic Caucus, June 30, 2018, http://www.civiccaucus.org/Reports/2018_Priority-Issues-Facing-Minnesota.html

301. "Looking Back, Thinking Ahead: Strengthening Minnesota's Public Policy Process", Civic Caucus, November 27, 2016, http://www.civiccaucus.org/Reports/PDF/2016_Public-Policy-Report_Looking-Back-Thinking-Ahead.pdf

302. "Fiscal Disparities Free List", Citizens League Fiscal Disparities Committee, 1968.

303. "New Formulas for Revenue Sharing in Minnesota", Citizens League, September 1, 1970, https://citizensleague.org/wp-content/uploads/2017/08/PolicyReportFiscalSept-70.pdf

304. David B. Walker, "It's a Conflict Between Generalists, Specialists",

*The Minneapolis Tribune*, February 7, 1969, 4.

305. "The Partnership's Work", Greater MSP, https://www.greatermsp.org/pages/what-we-do/

306. "About Us", Metro Cities (the Association of Metropolitan Municipalities), https://www.metrocitiesmn.org/about-us

307. Eric Roper and Torey Van Oot and Kavita Kumar, "Senate leader, governor consider aid plan for Mall of America", startribune.com, May 15, 2020, https://www.startribune.com/senate-leader-governor-consider-aid-plan-for-mall-of-america/570508462/

308. Ted Kolderie, "Getting After One of the Real Villains", Citizens League, 1970, https://irp-cdn.multiscreensite.com/564352d7/files/uploaded/Paul%20Gilje%20-%20Kolderie%20CL%20memo%20the%20the%20real%20villians.pdf

309. "Breaking the Tyranny of the Local Property Tax", Citizens League, March 20, 1969, 31-32.

310. "Common Good Common Ground", Citizens League, citizensleague.org.

311. Steven Dornfeld, "Metro tax-base-sharing bill squeezes through Senate", *Minneapolis Tribune*, June 2, 1971, 1.

312. Finlay Lewis, "Metro area to pool tax base under new law", *Minneapolis Tribune*, July 16, 1971, 1.

# References

Albert, Alan Dale. "Sharing Suburbia's Wealth: The Political Economy of Tax Base Sharing in Minnesota's Twin Cities Metropolitan Area". Harvard College. March 1979.

"Amicus Curiae: The Citizens League". Village of Burnsville v. Onischuk. (File Nos. 44232, 44253, Minn. Sup. Ct.) //mn.gov/law-library-stat/briefs/pdfs/222NW2d523ac1.pdf

"Amicus Curiae: The City of Bloomington"., Village of Burnsville v. Onischuk (File Nos. 44232, 44253, Minn. Sup. Ct.) //mn.gov/law-library-stat/briefs/pdfs/222NW2d523ac2.pdf

Bahl, Roy. "Regional Tax Base Sharing Possibilities and implications". *National Tax Journal*. 1 September 1976.

Berg, Tom. *Minnesota's Miracle: Learning from the Government that Worked*. University of Minnesota Press. Minneapolis. 2012

"Breaking the Tyranny of the Local Property Tax". Citizens League. March 20, 1969. https://citizensleague.org/wp-content/uploads/2017/08/PolicyReportFiscalMarch-69.pdf

*Burnsville '76: A Community History*. Bicentennial Heritage Committee. Burnsville, MN. 1976.

Village of Burnsville v. Onischuk. 301 Minn. 137, 222 N.W.2d 523 (1974)

Ceberio, Robert, and Ron Kase. "New Jersey Meadowlands A History". The History Press. Charleston, SC. 2015.

"The Citizens League Itself", *National Civic Review*, National Municipal League, July 1976, https://citizensleague.org/wp-content/uploads/2017/08/PolicyReportPublicPolicyJuly-76.pdf

Civic Caucus. "Evolution of 1971 Metropolitan Tax Base Sharing Law". September 14, 2012.

http://civiccaucus.org/discussions/2012/Gilje-Paul_09-14-12.html

"The Crisis Continues". 13th Annual Report. Advisory Commission on Intergovernmental Relations. February 1972. https://library.unt.edu/gpo/acir/Reports/information/M-73.pdf

DeBoer, Bob. "Gearing up for another30 years of tax-base sharing". *Minnesota Journal*. April 2007, 5. https://citizensleague.org/wp-content/uploads/2017/07/MNJournalApril2007.pdf

Ehlers, Robert L. "Minority Committee Report of the Fiscal Disparities Committee". Citizens League. March 14, 1969. https://citizensleague.org/wp-content/uploads/2017/08/PolicyReportFiscalMarch-69-2.pdf

"4,000,000 by 2000". the Joint Program. Twin Cities Metropolitan Planning Commission, December 1964

Gilbert, D. A. "Property Tax Base Sharing: An Answer to Central City Fiscal Problems?" *Social Science Quarterly*. Vol. 59. 1979.

Gilje, Paul. "Fiscal 'disparity' creates business 'parity'". *Minnesota Journal*. April 2007, 8. https://citizensleague.org/wp-content/uploads/2017/07/MNJournalApril2007.pdf

Gilje, Paul. "Minnesota's Metropolitan Tax Pool". *City*, Fall 1971. https://irp-cdn.multiscreensite.com/564352d7/files/uploaded/1971%20Minnesota%27s%20Metropolitan%20Tax%20Pool%20Gilje.pdf

Gilje, Paul. "Sharing of Tax Growth--Redefinitions". *Governmental Finance*, November 1977. https://irp-cdn.multiscreensite.com/564352d7/files/uploaded/Governmental%20Finance%20article%20Nov%201977%20by%20Gilje%20on%20TBS_jgxuigHlQIOhYbvqICuM.pdf

Gordon, Tracy. "Critics Argue The Property Tax Is Unfair. Do They Have A Point?". Tax Policy Center and Brookings Institution. March 9, 2020. https://www.taxpolicycenter.org/taxvox/critics-argue-property-tax-unfair-do-they-have-point.

"Iron Range Fiscal Disparities Study", Property Tax Division, Minnesota Deparment of Revenue, January 31, 2014, https://www.revenue.state.mn.us/sites/default/files/2018-11/iron_range_fiscal_disparities_study.pdf

Jackson, Kenneth T. Crabgrass Frontier: The Suburbanization of the United States. New York: Oxford University Press. 1985.

Kolderie, Ted. "Metropolitan Reorganization: The Fiscal Side". Upper Midwest Research and Development Council. December 1967. https://irp-cdn.multiscreensite.com/564352d7/files/uploaded/St.%20Thomas%20Conference%20discussion%20paper%20120867.pdf

Kolderie, Ted. *Thinking Out the How*, Beaver's Pond Press, Edina, MN. 2017.

"Looking Back, Thinking Ahead: Strengthening Minnesota's Public Policy Process", Civic Caucus, November 27, 2016, http://www.civiccaucus.org/Reports/PDF/2016_Public-Policy-Report_Looking-Back-Thinking-Ahead.pdf

Lyall, Katharine C. "Tax Base-Sharing: A Fiscal Aid Towards More Rational Land Use Planning". *Journal of the American Institute of Planners*. Vol. 41:2. 1975.

Marchione, Dr. William P. "Annexation Spurned: Brookline's 1873 Rejection of Boston".Brighton Allston Historical Society. http://www.bahistory.org/HistoryAnnexBrookline.html

McCutcheon v. State. Nos. TC-123,124 & 125 (Minn. T.C., Feb. 12, 1981)

*McCutcheon v. State*, No. 81-368 (Minn. Feb. 19, 1982).

"Metropolitan Area Park Needs." Citizens League, December 1964. https://citizensleague.org/wp-content/

uploads/2017/08/
PolicyReportLandDec-54.pdf

"Minnesota School Finance History: 1849-2019". Minnesota Department of Education, October 2019. https://webcache.googleusercontent.com/search?q=cache:Tuj4MSbZr90J:ht tps://education.mn.gov/mdeprod/idcplg%3FIdcService%3DGET_FILE%26dDocName%3D005211%26RevisionSelectionMethod%3Dlat estReleased%26Rendition%3Dprim ary+&cd=1&hl=en&ct=clnk&gl=us &client=firefox-b-1-d

"The 1979 Minnesota Tax-Increment Financing Act." *William Mitchell Law Review*: Vol. 7 : Iss. 3 . Article 2, https://open.mitchellhamline.edu/wmlr/vol7/iss3/2.

"New Formulas for Revenue Sharing in Minnesota". Citizens League. September 1, 1970. https://citizensleague.org/wp-content/uploads/2017/08/PolicyReportFiscalSept-70.pdf

Orfield, Myron. Metropolitics A Regional Agenda for Community and Stability. The Brookings Institution, 1997.

Orfield, Myron, and Nicholas Wallace. *The Minnesota Fiscal Disparities Act of 1971*. 33 Wm. Mitchell L. Rev. 591, 2007. *available at* https://scholarship.law.umn.edu/imo_studies/60/

Orfield, Myron, and Thomas Luce. "Regional Tax-Base Sharing: A Policy to Promote Fiscal Equity and Efficient Development Practices at the Metropolitan Scale". April 14-15, 2016. https://socialinnovation.usc.edu/wp-content/uploads/2017/09/Orfield-Tax-Base-Sharing-Final.pdf

Orfield, Myron, and Thomas F. Luce, Jr. *Region: Planning the Future of the Twin Cities*. University of Minnesota Press: Minneapolis, MN, 2010.

Orfield, Myron, and Thomas Luce, "NE Ohio-Cleveland Metropatterns", Institute on Metropolitan Opportunity, University of Minnesota Law School, 2008, https://scholarship.law.umn.edu/cgi/viewcontent.cgi?article=1024&context=imo_studies

"Overcoming Obstacles to the Purchase of Service, Citizens League, January 14, 1974, https://citizensleague.org/wp-content/uploads/2017/08/PolicyReportGovernmentJan-74.pdf

Plosila, Walter H. "Metropolitan Tax-Base-Sharing: Its Potential and Limitations". *Public Finance Quarterly*. Vol. 4. 1976.

"Priority Issues/Choices Facing Minnesotans", Civic Caucus, June 30, 2018, http://www.civiccaucus.org/Reports/2018_Priority-Issues-Facing-Minnesota.html

Rakow, Kaye, and Bob DeBoer. "How Fiscal Disparities Spreads Property Tax Base Around the Region". NAIOP Minnesota Chapter. https://citizensleague.org/wp-content/uploads/2017/08/PropertyTaxFiscalDisparities-Sharing-Wealth.pdf

Reschovsky, Andrew, and Gene Knaff. "Tax Base Sharing: An assessment of the Minnesota Experience". *Journal of the American Institute of Planners*. Vol. 43:4. 1977.

Reschovsky, Andrew. "An Evaluation of Metropolitan Area Tax Base Sharing". *National Tax Journal*. Vol. XXXIII:1. 1980.

San Antonio Indep. Sch. Dist. v. Rodriguez, 411 U. S. 1

Smith, Paul. "Tax Base Sharing: Local Response to Fiscal Federalism".

*Lincoln Institute of Land Policy.* Cambridge, MA, 1979.

"Statement on Changing the Fiscal Disparities Law". Citizens League. January 15, 1988. https:// citizensleague.org/wp-content/ uploads/2017/08/ PolicyReportFiscalJan-88.pdf

"Study of the Metropolitan Area Fiscal Disparities Program". Tischler/Bise. Bethesda, MD. February 13, 2012. https://www.revenue.state.mn.us/ sites/default/files/2018-11/fiscal-disparities-study-full-report.pdf

Swanson, Jared, and Steve Hinze. "Minnesota's Fiscal Disparities Law". February 2020. https://www.house. leg.state.mn.us/hrd/pubs/fiscaldis. pdf

"Tax Increment Financing Legislative Report". Office of the State Auditor. March 5, 2020. http://www.osa. state.mn.us/reports/tif/2018/ tifLegislative/tifLegislative_18_ report.pdf

Tiebout, Charles., University of Washington. "A Pure Theory of Local Expenditures". 1956. https:// en.wikipedia.org/wiki/ Tiebout_model

Trickey, Erick. "Why the Colonies' Most Galvanizing Patriot Never Became a Founding Father". *Smithsonian Magazine,* May 5, 2017. https://www. smithsonianmag.com/history/ transformative-patriot-who-didnt-become-founding-father-180963166/

"2018 Metropolitan Livable Communities Fund Annual Report". Metropolitan Council, August 2019. https://metrocouncil.org/ Communities/Services/Livable-Communities-Grants/LCA/2017-Livable-Communities-Annual-Report-(pdf).aspx

Vogt, Walter. "Tax Base Sharing: Implications from San Diego County". *Journal of the American Planning Association.* Vol. 45:2. 1979.

Walker v. Itasca County Auditor. 624 N.W.2d 599 (Minn. App. 2001).

Walker v. Itasca County Auditor, 642 N.W.2d 745 (Minn. 2002).

Weaver, Charles R. "Breaking the Tyranny of the Local Property Tax"., Proceedings of the Annual Conference on Taxation under the Auspices of the National Tax Association, Vol. 63 (1970).

"Why Not Buy Service?", Citizens League, September 1972, https:// citizensleague.org/wp-content/ uploads/2017/08/ PolicyReportGovernmentSept-72. pdf

Windhorst, John W., Jr. "The Minnesota Fiscal Disparities Law". July 1, 1975. https://irp-cdn.multiscreensite. com/564352d7/files/uploaded/ Paul%20Gilje%20-%20John%20 W.%20Windhorst%2C%20Jr.%20 analysis%20of%20TBS%20070175. pdf

# *About the author*

Paul Gilje was serving as staff to the Citizens League Fiscal Disparities Committee in 1968. F. Warren Preeshl shared with Gilje his suggestion for tax-base sharing at dinner before the committee's meeting on December 12, 1968. Gilje wrote the committee report recommending tax-base sharing. He followed progress of the proposal through the Legislature, administrative implementation, court challenges, and efforts to curtail or repeal the law. Gilje testified before the Minnesota Tax Court in the Shakopee case. He prepared annual Citizens League analyses of tax-base sharing.

Born Towner, North Dakota, March 25, 1937; Graduate, Carrington, North Dakota, High School, 1955; Bachelor of Science, Journalism, Northwestern University, Evanston, IL, 1959; Master of Science, Journalism, Northwestern, 1960; Staff writer, *Minneapolis Star*, 1960-1964; Associate Director, Citizens League, 1964-1988; Director of stewardship and administrator, Prince of Peace Lutheran Church, Burnsville, MN, 1988-1993; Stewardship consultant, The Rogers Company, 1993-2000; Executive Director, Presbyterian Homes Foundation, 2000-2005; Executive Director, Civic Caucus, 2005-2017.

pagilje@comcast.net

www.ingramcontent.com/pod-product-compliance
Lightning Source LLC
Chambersburg PA
CBHW060451280326
41933CB00014B/2730